"I think rock and roll is folk music, hip-hop is folk music, and the blues is definitely folk music. Folk music can't just be music that's not very loud, made by white people."

Steve Earle, p. 25

Contents

ON THE COVER

The cover of the "Folk" issue features the illustrated wizardry of Miami-based artist Brian Butler. Beloved for his Show Drawn series, in which he travels to gigs to live-draw what he sees, Butler turns that omniscient lens to the realm of folk music. And in the middle of the mass of people, performers, activists, and instrumentalists stands Pete Seeger — at once an accessible comrade and a mythical and musical guiding force.

NO DEPRESSION TEAM
Chris Wadsworth *Publisher*
Hilary Saunders *Managing Editor*
Stacy Chandler *Assistant Editor*
Sonja Nelson *Advertising*
Adam Kirr *Marketing and Social Media Manager*
Maureen Cross *Finance/Operations*

WEB nodepression.com
TWITTER & INSTAGRAM @nodepression
FACEBOOK facebook.com/nodepressionmag

GENERAL INQUIRIES
info@nodepression.com

ONLINE ADVERTISING
advertising@nodepression.com

SUBSCRIPTIONS
store.nodepression.com

JOURNAL DESIGN & PRODUCTION
Marcus Amaker
Printed in Nashville, Tennessee, by Lithographics Inc.

No Depression is part of the FreshGrass Foundation.
freshgrass.org
ISBN-13: 978-0-9994674-8-0
©2019, FreshGrass, LLC

Hello Stranger

BY HILARY SAUNDERS

Folk music was one of the first types of music I discovered on my own and fell in love with. In particular, folk songs of protest helped shape my musical tastes and career, not to mention a chunk of my entire value system.

It wasn't a particularly startling trajectory for a suburban kid coming of age during the Iraq invasion: Some early Bob Dylan albums led me to '60s folk revival records and Woodstock, which pointed back to Woody Guthrie and Pete Seeger. I met the contradictions of songs like the aggressive "Masters of War" and peaceful "Blowin' in the Wind" with equal measure — one would resonate more on one day and the other on the next. Crosby, Stills, Nash, and Young's "Ohio" was an early song I taught myself on guitar. The extra verses to "This Land is Your Land" are obviously my favorite and "We Shall Overcome" has always carried the weight of immediacy.

Yet, the older I got (and the more the internet came into our lives), the more I realized how narrow that scope of protest music really was, especially within the context of folk music as a whole. I wanted to hear the African American songs and spirituals that permeated the civil rights movement in the late 1950s and what women sang during the women's liberation movement into the 1980s.

These niches of folk music— not just limited to folk songs of protest — stoked

my interest in what folk music means other communities, both geographically and socially. In fact, one of my favorite musical discoveries of 2019 is a global community of electro-folk artists who blend the acoustic traditional and folk instruments of their own places with digital beats. Argentinian producer, instrumentalist, and teacher Barda's latest album, *Lembrança*, for example, hooked me with its slow groove of guitar, charango, and local shaker percussion

woven into a range of synth patters.

Broadening the context of folk music was a major goal for this issue. In fact, focusing on the "folks" of folk music themselves proved to be a strong guiding point. Stories in the "Folk" issue explore folk music from Spanish-language communities, Native American communities, and diasporic Yiddish-language communities. They highlight the folk music process that includes oral traditions carried from one generation of folks to another.

Of course, the issue also features many famous and beloved folk icons like Joni Mitchell and Guy Clark. New and established musicians like Trapper Schoepp, Tom Morello, and Steve Earle share their insights into this wide world of folk music, too.

Last, but certainly not least, we at *No Depression* are so thrilled to devote an entire section of the "Folk" issue to Pete Seeger in honor of his centennial this year. With incredible support from the FreshGrass Foundation, the American Folklife Center at the Library of Congress, and more, we were able to cover many facets of Pete's career — from the censorship he faced and fought to the environmental legacy he left in the Hudson River Valley to his enormous body of musical work. Like Pete did, we're looking both inside and outside of ourselves to gain a greater understanding of folk music and the world around us today.

THE FAMILY BUSINESS

The Thompsons, the Wainwrights, and others carry folk music across generations

by Katherine Turman

John and Lilly Hiatt

"With family, musically, you get something that you can't get with non-related musicians. Something quite special from the vocal blend to the feel that you have together, there's often something that you can't replicate with regular folks. But it can be fraught. So you can take that, or you can work with non-family members and it's much simpler, but it might not be as magical in some moments."
Teddy Thompson

My father is one of the greats to ever step on a stage
My mother has the most beautiful voice in the world
And I am betwixt and between, Sean Lennon, you know what I mean
Born to the manor, never quite clamoring free
It's family.

HE POIGNANT LYRICS ARE written and sung by Teddy Thompson, from the title track of 2014's *Family*, a collective album by the talented Thompson clan, headed by prolific patriarch Richard and ex-wife Linda. Richard came to prominence in the late 1960s with influential folk-rockers Fairport Convention; Linda is a stellar singer most successful with her former spouse, notably on their final album as husband and wife, 1982's beloved and acclaimed *Shoot Out the Lights*.

When Leo Tolstoy opined, "Happy families are all alike; every unhappy family is unhappy in its own way" in *Anna Karenina*, a multiple character study on the nature of family, he wasn't thinking of the particular plight of musical families, which, thanks to fame, ego, DNA, and just plain proximity, are fraught in their own particular ways. But a lot of great music comes out of that struggle, if *Family* and other records crafted by members of generational folk families are any indication.

"It's probably nature, something passed down, but it's true that there'd have to be some study of folk musicians separated at birth and when they got together in their 20s, did they have a nice vocal blend?" Teddy opines. "A great deal is what you learn in the decades when you're growing up. How we develop the way we speak and sound — the nuts and bolts and guts of our bodies, but it's also in large part what we hear, what we replicate, what we mimic.

So it's a bit of both, but there's no question when you hear The Carter Family sing together, or The Everly Brothers; you can't get non-related people to sing like that together."

In a 2010 article in *The Independent*, Carlene Carter — granddaughter of Mother Maybelle Carter, daughter of June Carter Cash, and stepdaughter of Johnny Cash — says whenever she considered leaving music, "there's just something in me that I can't stop. I have to get it out somehow and music is the most natural way for me. ... The songs that really speak to me, and the ones that I guess speak to other people, come from my roots or what I learned from osmosis. There's something about singing with family that's really cool." As a little girl, she remembers singing with relatives: "My aunt could tell if I was a little bit off — she'd give me this look, and if she nodded up I'd go up a little, and if she nodded down, I'd go down a little."

Which brings up the emotional aspect of being in a multi-generational singer-songwriter family. An iconic parent casts a long shadow. When your father is Bob Dylan, there's almost no surpassing that stature, and no way to avoid comparisons. Ditto the Guthries, Woody's son Arlo and his progeny. And Lucy Wainwright Roche has the added burden of both parents as musicians — her parents are Loudon Wainwright III and Suzzy Roche, and she's the half-sister of Rufus and Martha Wainwright, the kids of Kate McGarrigle. The familial experiences are as different as the music they make.

Nature vs. Nurture

Medical and academic studies have shown at least some connection between genetics and inherited musicality. Although the existing body of research is limited, *The American Journal of Human Genetics* published a study (Jarvela, et al. 2008) that shows

that certain chromosomes do indeed carry musical perception, pitch, memory, and more. Relatedly, another study (Peretz, et al. 2007) found that tone-deafness ("congenital amusia") is genetic as well.

From a qualitative perspective, singer-songwriter John Hiatt absolutely sees the hereditary nature of musical ability in his daughter Lilly, herself a singer-songwriter now: "I'm certain the long strands of the DNA, they reach far beyond the womb of the previous parentage. I mean, it's been proven in negative ways, as tendencies toward alcoholism. Lilly and I definitely kind of just fall together musically, we even play guitar very similarly; we use it in very much the same way."

In folk music, family groups like the Carters earned commercial and popular success as early as the 1920s with tight harmonies and mountain gospel music, bound together by blood, locale, and religion. When discussing musical families, Richard Thompson likes to go even further back in history, to Baroque composer Johann Sebastian Bach. Bach's father was director of musicians in Eisenach, Germany, and all his uncles were professional musicians. Bach himself had nine children who lived to adulthood; three became famous musically.

Describes Richard, "It was like, 'Here's the job; we need oratorios for next week, so can you get one done? I need 40 minutes of church music.' It's like the family business. It's just practical."

Teddy's song "Family" lays bare his feelings, practical or otherwise, about growing up in a musical family. The Brooklyn-based artist notes, "for my family, if you have something important to say you put it in a song, and there it is. The other [family members] can listen to it in their own time, but there's probably going to be much discussion about it. It's very passive-aggressive. For [the song "Family"] my mum is more

forthright and she said that she loved it, and my dad's not really that way."

All the family members brought their own songs to the project, but Teddy's younger sister, singer-songwriter Kamila Thompson, told *The New York Times* in 2014 that she would have preferred to sit out this *Family* affair, quipping, "Could I be like that one Osbourne who's not on the show, whose name no one knows?"

Even matriarch Linda felt the strain, telling the *Times* that she told her producer, "No pressure here — but my song has to be the best one."

Queried about the actual song "Family" in a separate interview, Richard says, "I thought it was a very good song. I thought it was kind of amusing in some ways, but it also brought up the difficulty of family as well. Every family has its struggles and its joys, and I think you have it all in that song."

For Richard's friend and contemporary Loudon Wainwright III, familial struggles seem more prominent than the joys, although both have played out on public stages. Sometimes they contain meanings less obvious to outsiders, like Rufus' "Lucy's Blue" (which he premiered on tour when sister Lucy Wainwright Roche opened for him). Their father has written at least two jarring songs about Rufus: "Rufus Is a Tit Man" (referring to baby Rufus during breastfeeding) and "A Father and a Son." And Martha wrote a self-aware song on her self-titled 2005 album inspired by her dad's habit of writing songs about the family, bluntly titled "Bloody Mother Fucking Asshole."

Sometimes, though, songs can be more like private conversations, like Rufus' "Martha" and "Little Sister." Most recently, in 2018, Loudon released "Meet the Wainwrights," a tune that features the children (Rufus, Martha, and Lucy), his sister (Sloan Wainwright), and his ex-wife (Suzzy Roche) and pokes fun at all of them with lyrics like, "Bein' a

Loudon Wainwright III

Wainwright can be a little much / But Martha and the bloody motherfuckin' asshole stay in touch." Not unsurprisingly, Loudon Wainwright III has often called his clan the "dysfunctional von Trapp family."

"If you want to know what's going on Loudon's life, just could go to one of his concerts and listen to his more recent songs, it's all in there," says Richard Thompson from his home in New Jersey. "I'm a lot more veiled. Loudon's heart is totally on his sleeve. We're always having a competition as to who's got the most musical offspring. I think he's winning at the moment by about one."

Independent Paths

John Hiatt and his daughter Lilly Hiatt are passionate performers but much more pacific relatives. The musical talents of Lilly, the middle child, initially "flew under the radar," her dad says. "She entered the high school talent show. We went to see her and she sang 'Wild Horses' and a John Prine song, 'Angel From Montgomery.' We'd never heard her sing. Our jaws dropped. It was like, 'Oh, she can sing and play the guitar.' Within two years she was off at college and immediately starting bands at the University of Denver," he says, with pride still in his voice. "She came home from college and drug a band back with her and stated that, 'You know, I'm going to do this for a living.' I said, 'Well, good luck,' he remembers with a laugh. "It's not easy."

Growing up, Lilly gained a love of music from her touring father, but also entertained a range of career paths. "I always wanted to be a musician. ... I always would say, 'I want to be this *and* a singer.' Like, I want to be marine biologist *and* a singer. I want to be a vet and a singer.'"

Family ties still tugged, though, and Lilly's most recent album, 2017's *Trinity Lane,* showcases those connections.

"Imposter," a song about her dad and birth mother, is a tender tune that John says made him cry.

Arlo Guthrie had a bit of similar experience in finding his path. "I knew I wanted to play music, but I had no intention of making it a career. I wanted to be a forest ranger. Neither of my younger siblings, Joady or Nora, ever were expected to follow our dad's lead. We were really encouraged to do whatever seemed natural and follow our own ideas of what seemed right for us individually."

While Arlo isn't a forest ranger and Lilly isn't a vet, neither really leaned on their dads for assistance either. In fact, Lilly didn't show her father any of her original songs until she was 21. "It was late," she acknowledges, "but he did give me honest criticism, to the point where I've definitely learned when the time is to show him things or not, because that's a really close relationship. If you want that kind of honest feedback from someone close to you, you have to be, like, prepared. Right? [Feedback] is effective in a different way than somebody who's a little more objective, I think. When it's a family member, you can definitely take that to heart. I listened to everything he said. It was clear that he was supporting me."

Richard Thompson has a different story. His own dad played a little guitar, but "he would try to discourage me. Which is kind of sad, really," he recalls. "I mean, with my kids, I probably, you know, under-encouraged them through the years. I'm sorry about that. I should have actually encouraged them a bit more. I've been careful to strike the right balance to say, 'That's great. You know that you're a great musician.' But also to say, 'You know, you're not quite there yet. Keep trying.'" That said, he adds with a laugh, "I don't know how much what I say affects my kids. Sometimes I think they just ignore me. Maybe that's just as well! I see my kids as very accomplished, smarter than I am or certainly than I

Arlo Guthrie

was at their age. Way more canny about the music business and all that stuff. I see them as fairly complete artists at this point."

Subtext and the Sublime

When members of a band who aren't related write songs, tour, and argue about music and then (perhaps) work things out, it can be painful, but it's not always heart-rending, and it doesn't always reach back into and reignite childhood hurts or memories. When it's family, Teddy Thompson believes, "there's always a subtext, because you know too much about each other and it's very loaded. Or could be, potentially. With strangers, it's just 'You're not playing it right,' we're not really talking about when you set fire to the living room rug when you were 7."

However, Teddy muses further on family harmony — the musical type, that is: "With family, musically, you get something that you can't get with non-related musicians. Something quite special from the vocal blend to the feel that you have together, there's often something that you can't replicate with regular folks. So there's that. But it can be fraught. So you can take that, or you can work with non-family members and it's much simpler, but it might not be as magical in some moments."

There was magic on *Family* — five members contributed songs. But doing an album was definitely not all about the music, as Teddy now understands. "In retrospect, I realized that, really what I was trying to do was get my family back together in some way; I was trying to repair something from my childhood, which I didn't realize until it was done. I thought that I was doing something for everyone, but, really, I was doing something for me. Trying to repair some wounds and get my parents back together," he says with a laugh. "As a child of divorce it was a repair job. In some way

it was therapeutic."

The Guthrie clan honors their patriarch, the writer of many chestnuts — including one of America's best-known folk songs, "This Land Is Your Land" — via the name of their record label, Rising Son. Yet Arlo, 71, says, "I don't know if [folk] actually is more generational than, say, bluegrass or gospel or a myriad of other forms of music. But I was captured by the traditional styles I heard as a kid. My first love was ragtime music, and I still love it. I had access to my father's record collection, so I was influenced early. He had everything imaginable, from orchestral music, to Dixieland, blues, sea shanties, cowboy ballads ... even political speeches, all on records."

"Keeping family tradition alive" seems to be a Guthrie family motto. But musician Annie Guthrie, Arlo's middle daughter — and her siblings — felt they had a choice to not follow in the family's folk footsteps. "Some of my favorite music growing up was metal, punk, rap, and rock. I did not live in a folk bubble," she says. "My parents were actually very cool about tolerating our musical tastes. My dad took me to see Men Without Hats when I was 8 years old. It's pretty hard to be a rebel in this family. I'd have to be an attorney or accountant."

While Arlo, like his father, wrote an iconic song — "Alice's Restaurant" — neither Annie nor her siblings seem to feel that they're living in the shadow of those patriarchs. "I am honored to be a member of such an incredible family. I have no interest in being the next Woody or Arlo Guthrie," Annie says. "I am just me, take it or leave it."

Family — whether musical, fraught, both, or neither — is hard to escape. When Teddy Thompson is asked about working again with family members on music, the answer is swift, though delivered with a laugh: "Oh God, no!" But he doubles back with, "I mean, probably ... ." Indeed, as he so perfectly summarizes in song: "It's family." ∎

14

Trapper and Tanner Schoepp

STEPHEN BLOCH

EXTENDING THE LINE

Folk traditions inspire Trapper Schoepp's songwriting

By Joshua M. Miller

FOR MILWAUKEE-BASED singer-songwriter Trapper Schoepp, storytelling is part of his DNA. His grandfather loved telling tall tales, and growing up in western Wisconsin close to the Minnesota border and the Mississippi River, Trapper spent much of his free time channeling his spirit and telling stories about the world around him.

"I grew up in a small Wisconsin town where everyone felt like characters from a Coen Brothers movie," he says. "My friends and I couldn't help but spinning these mini narratives about my town. There's pieces of me in all the characters I write about."

When Schoepp started using some of those stories in song, he turned to his brother Tanner to help bring his vision to life. Tanner has been the only constant in Trapper's band, playing bass and contributing backing vocals.

"It's like we have the same make and model instrument, genetically speaking," Tanner says.

Between the familial and geographic influences, it's no surprise that Trapper believes so strongly in the folk tradition of taking what one generation started and finishing it. Or as he calls it, "extending the line."

"When I think about music, I think about it in terms of it constantly changing and evolving and moving with time," he says.

The Dylan's in the Details

Schoepp extended the line in a high-profile way on his latest album, *Primetime Illusion*, when he turned some of Bob Dylan's unused lyrics about Wisconsin into a song.

He shares the songwriting credit with Dylan, as the legendary songwriter gave the young upstart his blessing (thanks to a series of long-shot emails from Schoepp's managerial team to Dylan's). After adding a melody and chorus to Dylan's lyrical sketch, Schoepp recorded the song, which he titled "On, Wisconsin."

Schoepp first noticed the unused Dylan lyrics while looking through a 2017 issue of *Rolling Stone*. The story broke news of an auction listing (with a $30,000 asking price) and included a transcript of the original handwritten lyrics that detail Dylan's brief time living in Wisconsin, name-dropping places and things associated with the state.

He was even more impressed when he saw "11/20/61" scribbled down as the date the lyrics were written — it was the first day Dylan stepped into the Columbia Recording Studio to start work on his debut album.

"It probably took Dylan less than 10 minutes to write those two pages of lyrics about Wisconsin," Schoepp says. "It recalls the playfulness of Woody Guthrie's lyrics and other folk singers Dylan would have been listening to at that time. To me, it feels like a travelogue."

Daniel Holter, a sound engineer at Wire & Vice studio in Wauwatosa, produced "On, Wisconsin" before turning the rest of the album's

Trapper Schoepp

production over to Wilco's Pat Sansone.

With its waltz-like tempo, the song mirrors the rhythm of its train-riding narrator who longs for Wisconsin.

"We're great admirers of Dylan, so Trapper's inspiration to set the lyrics to music seemed in line with how any folk song is adapted over time," says Tanner. "It felt apropos of our fandom and state citizenry and was exciting to record even without the foresight that Bob would approve a co-write."

Trapper vividly recalls the first time he listened to Bob Dylan as a teenager. He lay on the red checkered couch in his parents' basement, recovering from a herniated disc he got from a BMX bicycle accident. To pass the time, he began watching a BMX-themed movie.

Suddenly, Dylan's "Hurricane" erupted from the TV's speakers, marked by its momentous A-minor chord. His jaw dropped. He was astounded by the conviction in Dylan's voice and lyrics and instantly wanted to learn more about him.

"The song shook my existence," Trapper says. "That A-minor chord changed the direction of my whole life."

Years later, Schoepp got to have his own shot at being a touring musician, traveling around the world and opening for acts such as The Jayhawks and The Wallflowers (led by Bob Dylan's son, Jakob) and headlining his own shows. "Jakob has given me some really good advice about music being cyclical and staying the course," Schoepp says. "For a kid who grew up in the '90s, it doesn't get much cooler than singing 'One Headlight' with Jakob Dylan."

Folk Traditions

Throughout *Primetime Illusion*, as he has on previous albums, Schoepp honors and builds upon folk traditions he learned colloquially through his family and academically as a student at the University of Wisconsin-Milwaukee. There, Schoepp earned a certificate in rock and roll studies that was heavy on analyzing early folk and blues music. He decided early in his career, though, that it was important to modernize these folk traditions with his own vision.

In particular, the old family ties and oral storytelling proved rich fodder. "Run, Engine, Run," the title track from Schoepp's 2011 album, for example, was inspired by the last gift his story-loving grandfather gave him, a 1964 Mercedes-Benz.

"He was a salt-of-the-earth South Dakota farmer who worked till his last day," Schoepp says. "The song was inspired by the car, but it's really about keeping his story and spirit alive through song. What could be more folky than that?"

Additionally, "Ballad of Olof Johnson," off his 2016 Brendan Benson-produced album *Rangers & Valentines*, tells the incredible tale of his great-great-great grandfather's first winter in America.

The song is "emblematic of my grandpa's storytelling," says Schoepp. "Olof was his grandpa, so he provided a link to us in that story's chain. It's hard to separate the fact from fiction with a story like that, but that gray area is where my songwriting exists."

According to family lore, the elder forefather migrated to the US from Sweden around 1900. During a particularly harsh South Dakotan winter, he managed to make a shelter for himself by digging a hole in the ground and flipping his wagon over it as a makeshift roof.

"It's a story of perseverance, immigration, and family," Schoepp says. "Having a couple Schoepp voices present through that helps drive home the story. I don't think that story would have the same effect if it wasn't told by two brothers and [sung] by two brothers."

Present Tense

In another parallel to Dylan's early oeuvre, many songs on *Primetime Illusion*, which came out in January, comment on the current political and personal disillusionment Schoepp sees in America.

"I see so much hate and so many lies told on a daily basis. It's literally something you would sit down in a movie theater and watch unfolding before your eyes," he says. "It almost does feel like an illusion. Like a magic trick that our president is playing over the people. We all have that same level of disillusionment in our own personal lives as well, whether that's heartbreak in our relationships or if it's unfulfilled hopes and dreams."

One of the most challenging songs

Schoepp wrote was "What You Do to Her," a song featuring guest vocals from Nicole Atkins in which he addresses the onslaught of sexual assault allegations coming to light in conjunction with the #MeToo movement.

"I feel like men have stood on the sidelines of this issue for far too long," he says. "It affects people in every community and every town whether they'd like to admit it or not. It has a ripple effect. My generation needs to face this issue head on if we want change.

"Men have to be more vocal and amplify these kinds of stories, and we have to use our voices and not cower in fear. The song was challenging in that I wanted to tell the story in a respectful way that was sensitive to those who have been through these kinds of assaults."

Schoepp started writing the song on Oct. 3, 2017, the day after his music hero Tom Petty died.

"I think I was looking to write something to chase away the demons and let the light back in," he says. "I was thinking about Tom Petty and extending that line and keeping his swagger alive in my music."

Just a couple days later, news broke of the stunning sexual assault allegations against movie producer Harvey Weinstein. "I ended up taking Tuesday's idea and combining it with Thursday's idea, which was writing numerous verses inspired by this monster, for lack of a better word, and these allegations against him."

Whether through songs like "On, Wisconsin" or "What You Do to Her," Schoepp strives to use folk music as a vessel to chronicle and make sense of the world around him. Storytelling through song provides a way to document and preserve lessons and knowledge for future generations. And working alongside his brother has helped solidify his special take on such a long and immense folk tradition.

For Schoepp, it's important to keep extending the line and keep the songs and stories alive.

"The generational passing of songs and stories is important to keep this tradition going," he says. "As this kind of music becomes more of a niche, I think there's a weight for young artists like me to keep it alive. It all comes back to the folk process." ∎

Steve Earle

Guy Clark

OLD FRIENDS

Steve Earle on Guy Clark's songs, life, and legacy
by Chuck Armstrong

Steve Earle & The Dukes

HEN HE LEAVES this life, Steve Earle will depart with only one regret, he writes in the liner notes of his latest album: "I never wrote a song with Guy Clark."

The new record, *Guy*, is a tribute to his late mentor and friend. This regret is something Earle keeps close to his chest, but on a bright and chilly day in New York City, he's ready to reminisce about that friendship.

Earle picks Caffe Reggio for this conversation, finding warmth in the cappuccinos and creaky chairs of one of the oldest coffee shops in New York.

"The very first espresso machine probably in the entire United States was here," he says immediately as he walks through the door. Chances are he's right, considering the café's founder, Domenico Parisi, first introduced the Italian cappuccino stateside back in the 1920s.

Earle talks loud enough for the whole café to hear, though no one seems to mind; his voice blends in with the steam wands and coffee grinders, along with the chatter and car horns outside on MacDougal Street. It's not dissimilar to the start of the title track of Earle's album from 2000, *Transcendental Blues* — a miscellany of seemingly random sounds that come together for an unforgettable song.

Caffe Reggio is in Greenwich Village, situated between Earle's home on Bleecker Street and Washington Square Park, and about a five-minute walk from one of his favorite places to record, Electric Lady Studios. Earle's neighborhood is often lauded as the epicenter of the 20th-century folk music movement, but he knows any discussion or appreciation of the genre can't be dominated by New York City.

In an effort to broaden that discussion and appreciation, Earle released *Townes* in 2009, a covers album that pays tribute to his friend, mentor, and fellow Texan and Tennessean Townes Van Zandt. Now, 10 years later, Earle continues celebrating the folk influence that existed far from the Village with a record that salutes another friend, mentor, and Texan and Tennessean: Guy Clark.

Musical Kinship

When Earle discusses folk music — or any genre for that matter — he does so from a deep well of personal experience creating his own music. "I started playing guitar at 11 years old," says Earle. "My mom's half brother, he gave me my first Dylan album, he introduced me to the Stones, Beatles, he gave me my first guitar, my first blunt, my first shot of dope."

Throughout his early years, Earle couldn't get away from listening to and being influenced by artists like Clark and Van Zandt, who seemed ubiquitous in the folk music scene in Texas. Before they would become his friends and mentors, they were the very musicians he aspired to be like. Earle released his first EP, *Pink & Black,* in 1982, and then on March 5, 1986, he topped the country charts with his Grammy-nominated debut studio album, *Guitar Town*. Though his career was only beginning, it was impossible to deny the lasting effect Earle was already having on the music scene.

Earle's outlaw lifestyle grew in proportion with his stature in the world of outlaw country. In the early-'90s, he was arrested for possession of heroin, and, later, for possession of cocaine and weapons; Earle was sentenced to a year in jail and released after 60 days.

As he kicked his drug habit and stayed out of handcuffs, Earle's musical output continued. Since the release of *Transcendental Blues*, he's released nine more full-lengths, with one of those paying homage to Van Zandt and the most recent, *Guy*, released via New West in March, applauding the life and influence of Clark.

"When I made the Townes record, I knew in the back of my mind that I'd make a Guy record one day," Earle says, pausing to pick up his chain wallet that keeps slipping out of his pocket. "I never talked to him about it, though."

The 16-song album, recorded in a mere six days, features some of Earle's favorite Guy Clark songs. Sometimes Earle and his band, The Dukes, put their own spin on the original material: They electrify "Dublin Blues," for example, and inject "Sis Draper" with a jolt of energy and faster tempo. Other times, though, Earle and company stay true to those early recordings, like the old-school "L.A. Freeway" or the

heartbreakingly beautiful "The Randall Knife." No matter what, though, throughout *Guy*, Earle's perfectly ragged voice stands in endearing contrast to Clark's smoother vocals.

The sincere reverence and acclaim for Clark is most notable on the closing track, "Old Friends," the title track to Clark's 1988 record, originally written by Clark and his wife, Susanna, as well as Richard Dobson. Earle's rendition lives up to its legacy, with Rodney Crowell and Emmylou Harris contributing vocals, along with friends Terry Allen, Jerry Jeff Walker, Jo Harvey Allen, Shawn Camp, Verlon Thompson, Mickey Raphael, Jim McGuire, and Gary Nicholson all lending a hand to the song as well.

The only track not recorded specifically for *Guy* is "The Last Gunfighter Ballad," a cover Earle originally made for a private tribute to Clark that later ended up on the 2011 compilation album, *This One's For Him: A Tribute to Guy Clark*.

"My one suggestion to Steve was that he had to put that version on the album," says Crowell, a fellow follower of Clark. "I don't think there's a better cover of one of Guy's songs."

Earle stays true to the simple arrangement of "The Last Gunfighter Ballad," the closing track on Clark's second LP, 1976's *Texas Cookin'*. "I didn't do anything on [*Texas Cookin'*]," says Earle, who had met and befriended Clark by the time that album was recorded, "but I hung out for every minute of it. The main thing I

contributed was I had a bag of really good Colombian red marijuana. I'll never forget, we were somewhere in the mixing process and I rolled up a joint and said, 'Guy, this is the last of the red bud.'"

Mimicking a stoned Clark swaying in his chair, Earle continues, "Guy looked at me and said, 'Good.' And that was the last night of *Texas Cookin'*."

A Seat at the Table

Crowell's suggestion to Earle about "The Last Gunfighter Ballad" wasn't a random interaction between the two artists; their friendship goes back decades, and is inseparable from their own relationships with Clark.

A Grammy award-winning artist himself, Crowell released his debut LP, *Ain't Living Long Like This*, in 1978, and just a couple of years after Earle's success with *Guitar Town*, he celebrated five No. 1 singles from his 1988 record, *Diamonds & Dirt*.

Somewhere in the midst of moving to Nashville and releasing his first album, Crowell distinctly remembers meeting Clark.

"I shared a house with Skinny Dennis and Richard Dobson, two old folkies," recalls Crowell. "We were roommates, and I came in one afternoon, I don't know where I'd been, and there was a party going on. It was the middle of the day and Guy was passed out in my bed. His cowboy boots were hanging off the end of the bed and he was facedown.

[His wife] Susanna told me that he had a bad hangover and he needed to borrow my bed. That was my first encounter with him."

A man with an extraordinary memory, Crowell also vividly calls to mind when he first ran into Earle. Instead of his bedroom, though, this encounter was at a Nashville staple, Bishop's Pub.

"I met Steve when he was 17 years old when he came into Nashville. He was already a fully formed songwriter," Crowell says. "The songs that he brought in that I first heard really outdid what I brought to town. This guy already had a seat at the table."

Earle had fallen in love with music in Texas, befriended Van Zandt in Houston, and hitchhiked all the way to Nashville for one major reason: "One of the things at the top of my list was to meet Guy Clark," Earle confesses. "I knew Townes, but I needed to know Guy."

When a 19-year-old Earle walked into Bishop's Pub one night in 1974, he remembers seeing Richard Dobson behind the bar and being told that Clark was in the back. "I walked into the pool room and there was Guy and Susanna and Jim Stafford and Deborah Allen," he recalls. "I had this cowboy hat on that everyone recognized me with, a black, 3X beaver American hat. Guy leaned over a shot, looked up and saw me and said, 'I like your hat.' He took the shot and started talking to me and found out I knew Townes. From that point on I was kind of 'in.'"

A few years later, Earle was invited to sing background vocals with Crowell and Emmylou Harris on Clark's 1975 debut LP, *Old No. 1*, and he was welcomed into Clark's writing process.

"Guy showed me how he laid his songs out on paper. He saw me writing with a pen once and he told me to write with a pencil," Earle says, smiling. "People would ask him how he writes songs and he would always say, 'With a pencil and big eraser.'"

That simple skill was crucial for a prolific songwriter like Clark. As Crowell remembers his own interactions with him, he always recalls how hard a worker Clark was. "With Guy, writing songs was like sitting at the workbench," he says. "I understood that you'd get there with hard work and dedication and paying close attention to the craft. You stay up all night, then get up and go to work the next day. Guy was infinitely valuable."

Earle can't help but agree, adding, "He would always say, 'Listen to this song,' to me or Rodney. If he had a song that he thought I should hear or Rodney should hear or Neil Young should hear, he'd make us listen to it. Attention to detail was everything in the way he wrote. It's one of those things I've carried through my career and life."

While other young musicians might have been dying to be the next Beatles or Rolling Stones, guys like Crowell and Earle, influenced by the storytelling deftness of Clark and Van Zandt, seemed more comfortable in the folk tradition. Sure, their albums may have had a bit more twang to them than what was

coming out of coffeehouses in New York City, but their commitment to portraying life through song was just as, if not more, authentic and powerful.

"We'd sit around and [Clark] would play tapes of Dylan Thomas reading poetry and he'd say we need to make our words sound like we have a command of language like this," Crowell remembers. "That was exactly what the doctor ordered for somebody who wanted to write songs."

Folk Focus

Both Earle and Crowell are adamant that folk music can't be confined to the streets of New York. Though artists like Bob Dylan, Tom Paxton, and Buffy Sainte-Marie are inextricably connected to the 1960s folk scene in Greenwich Village, even their contributions were in part influenced by their lives outside of the city. Dylan grew up and started playing music in Minnesota, Paxton studied drama at the University of Oklahoma before making his way to the East Coast, and Sainte-Marie was born on the Piapot Plains Cree First Nation Reserve in Saskatchewan and later studied Eastern philosophy in Massachusetts.

"Folk music was always much bigger [than New York]," says Earle. "Chicago had a scene. Minneapolis. Boston. Houston. Any place that had a college, because if you had a college, it meant you had a coffeehouse."

Crowell concurs, saying, "I wasn't moved by the stuff in Greenwich Village

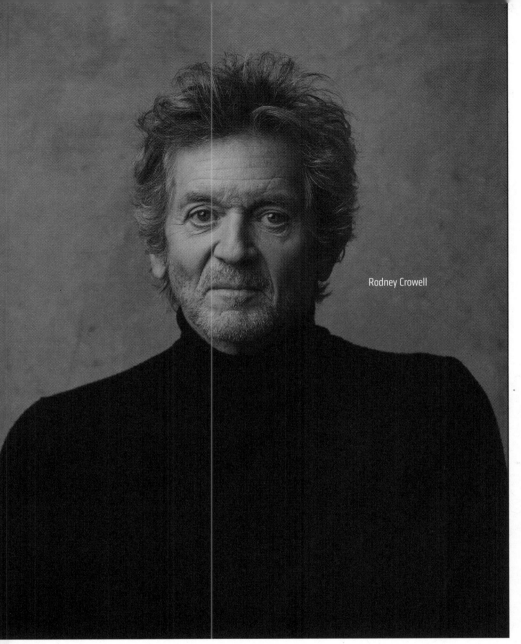

Rodney Crowell

until I started to understand it through Dylan. Dylan wasn't trying to win over a large crowd with how smooth he could deliver his stuff. This was about delivering from the gut. That's how I always understood folk music, and that's why Steve will always be connected with folk music."

Earle relishes that connection, honoring it with historical documents like *Townes* and *Guy*. He brings a sense of eternity to these bodies of work, forever expanding the reaches of the folk tradition.

"For me, folk music is always much bigger than what you or I think or talk about," admits Earle. "Hip-hop is folk music. Two kids unpacking a piece of digital gear that they barely understand and they start to push buttons is not that

much different than a dental student picking up a five-string banjo in 1948 and going to Washington Square Park. It's an experiment. If it isn't written down, if it isn't on a piece of paper, if the musician can't read music, it's folk music. That's the definition, it's handed down by an oral tradition."

He continues, "It's not about the kind of guitar you use or how you pick the strings. ... Now, I know all of those things and I protect them, but I think folk music is part of rock and roll. I think rock and roll is folk music, hip-hop is folk music, and the blues is definitely folk music. Folk music can't just be music that's not very loud, made by white people."

Like his mentors before him, Earle has no interest in compartmentalizing folk music, or his own diverse legacy for

that matter. Clark and Van Zandt never liked having labels placed on them, and neither does Earle. What he is more concerned with is, as he puts it, the integrity of his craft, but he's quick to admit that even in his own experiences with Clark and Van Zandt, that integrity can manifest itself in varied ways.

"The difference between Townes Van Zandt and Guy Clark is like the difference between Jack Kerouac and Allen Ginsberg," Earle says confidently. "One lived to not be very old, was never particularly disciplined, and didn't do much the last couple of decades of his life. That's Kerouac and Townes. Allen, he taught and wrote and left a body of work and it was incredible. If you ever doubt that, go buy a copy of the collected poems of Allen Ginsberg. It will blow your fucking mind. He wrote right to the end. Guy did, too. He started co-writing with younger artists just to keep going. He never stopped writing."

For all the different projects that take up space in his brain and on his schedule, Earle tends to favor a similar commitment to making writing a priority above all else.

"The only time I ever came close to stopping playing music was when my drug habit got out of hand and I didn't even have a guitar," he says solemnly as the final drops of his cappuccino make their way down a graying beard that stretches to his chest. "But I believe I was spared for a reason. I think I was put here to be a songwriter, so I write songs. I think any good I'm going to do in this world will start with that." ■

Clouds
Joni mitchell

50 YEARS IN THE CLOUDS

The sublime voice and songwriting of Joni Mitchell

by Caryn Rose

HEN DISCUSSING Joni Mitchell's body of work, her second album, 1969's *Clouds*, is almost always glossed over. No one claims it as their favorite Joni record, as it, understandably, lives in the shadows of albums like *Blue*, *Ladies of the Canyon*, and *Court and Spark*. But *Clouds* deserves a place of honor not just because it contains chestnuts like "Chelsea Morning" and "Both Sides, Now," but also because it was a critical artistic stepping stone, without which those subsequent efforts — and in fact, the total arc of Mitchell's career — might not have manifested in the same way. Fifty years after its original release, *Clouds* remains a milestone of a female artist asserting her equal rights and talent as well as a signpost in the '60s folk movement, even if its creator felt that she was no longer working or writing within that particular tradition.

Clouds greets listeners with a self-portrait of Mitchell staring boldly out from the cover. The image is not unattractive, but it isn't the soft-focus photo typical for female artists in the early-'60s. Instead, Mitchell went her own way, controlling the image as well as the arrangements and production for her music. The credits for Mitchell on *Clouds* read: "Composer, cover art, guitar, keyboards, producer, vocals." She allowed Stephen Stills to play occasional bass and guitar where needed. Paul Rothchild shares a production credit on one song, and Henry Lewy, the man who became her longtime partner behind the board across 13 albums, has the engineering credit. In 2019, this is not terribly remarkable, but in 1969, it was exceptional, deliberate, and hard-won, even with supportive managers Elliot Roberts and David Geffen standing alongside her. In that era women did not often march into the recording studio of their choice, then direct the recording of material written and performed by themselves, carrying a guitar strung to their own tunings.

Getting there was a carefully calculated strategy on Mitchell's part, pieces she put in motion once she made the decision to focus on music. At age 22, she moved from Toronto to Detroit, and just two years later (when she and her first husband Chuck Mitchell divorced), she left for New York City, building her career as she went along, the steps becoming more deliberate as she gained momentum. In New York, she set herself to writing four songs a day and booked herself into coffee houses all over Greenwich Village. The quality of her songwriting had a long reach, garnering even more admiration than her stunning vocal range. Established artists such as Judy Collins, Tom Rush, and Ian & Sylvia wanted to use her work.

Running the Show

Mitchell arrived in Los Angeles in 1968 and headed for Laurel Canyon. In her house on Lookout Mountain, she put together her first album, known both as *Joni Mitchell* and as *Song to a Seagull*, released in March 1968 and produced by her friend David Crosby. This was another calculated move on both Mitchell's and Crosby's part, as Mitchell explained to *Mojo* in 1994: "His instincts were correct: he was going to protect the music and pretend to produce me. So we just went for the performance, with a tiny bit of sweetening. I think perhaps without David's protection the record company might have set some kind of producer on me who'd have tried to turn an apple into an orange. And I don't think I would have survived that."

That debut did well enough, peaking at No. 189 on the *Billboard* 200, to afford Mitchell the opportunity for *Clouds*. But she bided her time, despite having enough songs ready for three albums. "I could have recorded a year ago," she told *Broadside* in 1968. "But I waited until I was in a bargaining position. And Judy Collins' album was the thing that really put me in a position where I could get the things I really want." (Collins released the first recorded version of "Both Sides, Now" on her 1967 album *Wildflowers*, where the track won the Grammy for Best Folk Performance in 1968. Mitchell would claim the same award for *Clouds* in 1969.)

Mitchell went into the studio to work on *Clouds* with Paul Rothchild, a producer pre-assigned to her who was best known for his work with The Doors. However, they didn't work well together, so when Rothchild left the studio for two weeks on a Doors-related errand, Mitchell persuaded engineer Henry Lewy to help her record the entire album in his absence.

Her confidence and self-determination proved effective: *Clouds* sounded better, stronger, and clearer than her debut. It sounded like Mitchell was running the show.

Folk and Not Folk

"I was a folksinger as Joni Anderson," Mitchell told biographer David Yaffe. "As soon as I became Joni Mitchell, I was no longer a folksinger. Once I started to write my music, that's not folk music." But despite her own assertions, *Clouds* and other albums from her early years are regularly claimed as folk due to their reliance on acoustic instrumentation and emphasis on songs that were deeply personal and told stories.

These songs remain transformational because at the time, women were not writing in such candid, unabashed terms about their love lives. Mitchell had no qualms about detailing her affairs, and she did so not with remorse, but with great forgiveness and affection.

While there isn't as clear a thematic line on *Clouds* as on her debut, it is sonically cohesive. On *Clouds*, she uses the silence around the songs to emphasize the emotions, whether flavors of shade ("I Think I Understand"), light ("Chelsea Morning"), or drama ("The Fiddle and the Drum"). This album is Mitchell and her voice, along with her guitar — and in one case (the Tolkien-esque "I Think I Understand"), a trumpet.

Songs like "That Song about the Midway" are vivid and memorable. Here, Mitchell employs a lilting melody that conveys the free-wheeling feeling brought on by the circus rolling into town. The casualness of her vocal delivery seems to imply that Mitchell isn't all that invested in the gentleman described in the song. Also of note is her ability to vocally shape words to make them fit into the melody she's specified, like "another town," or "worth the price." It's elegant and gentle, as Mitchell's innate faculty with phrasing and swing foreshadows her later jazz-influenced sound.

Other songs on *Clouds* became commercially successful fan favorites. Although Mitchell later downplayed "Chelsea Morning" by saying, "It's a very sweet song, but I don't think of it as part of my best work," the track stands well within the canon of great songs about New York City. Mitchell's authoritative chords and brisk delivery invoke the sounds of the traffic she's singing about, with her crisp, impeccable vocals making for a solid radio hit in 1969.

A standout showcase for those vocals is the album's protest song, "The Fiddle and the Drum." It's presented a cappella, the melody reminiscent of an old mountain ballad. The pause it creates at its finish sets the stage for the album's final track, the standout "Both Sides, Now." Mitchell's authoritative chords open the song, then slide back to let her voice come to the forefront. Her delivery is definitive, and singular; no one has ever sung "Both Sides, Now" the way its author did. She inhabits the words with warmth and gravity. She is telling a story, summarizing the essence of having a human experience, which is likely the reason for its enduring popularity.

"Both Sides, Now" has been performed by a diverse body of artists, including Glen Campbell, Herbie Hancock, Sara Bareilles, and Hurray for the Riff Raff's Alynda Segarra.

Kristian Matsson, the Swedish singer-songwriter who performs under the name The Tallest Man on Earth, included "Both Sides, Now" in his YouTube video series "The Light in Demos" in 2017. His version evokes a feeling of stardust similar to that of the original, and Matsson carefully, intentionally uses space with the vocals and interlaces them with delicate horns that escalate gently until the end. He introduces the song by asking, "What is the best song in the world?" before answering himself, with an air of obviousness: "It's 'Both Sides, Now' by Joni Mitchell."

Matsson, whose fifth album *I Love You. It's a Fever Dream.* was released in April, discovered Mitchell's music as a self-declared teenaged "weirdo."

"I felt like I was connecting to Joni because of how she writes, the melodies and the lyrics, they are so unique, and in the best sense, weird," he says. "But they sound so natural. And that is with different weird guitar tunings and melodies that ... how could you ever think about some of these lines? They just tumbled out of her, and they sound also so natural, and it was extremely inspiring."

Too Much Hiss

Despite how much the record was lauded in many quarters, two voices of the counterculture Mitchell was part of at the time were outright dismissive of *Clouds*. Ben Fong-Torres wrote in *Rolling Stone*, "Miss Mitchell is just a singer who sounds like Joan Baez or Judy Collins" and "Joni Mitchell is a fresh, incredibly beautiful innocent/experienced girl/woman" in a story that devoted more words to the decor of her house in Laurel Canyon than to her music.

Robert Christgau of the *Village Voice* gave the album a C, complained that Mitchell's voice sounded "malnourished," and bemoaned the absence of David Crosby as one of the reasons he found the album lacking. (Crosby later admitted that he not only had had no idea what he was doing as producer, but also that he in fact bungled the job, according to Yaffe's *Reckless Daughter*: "I hadn't recorded it well enough. I had allowed too much noise — too much signal-to-noise ratio — too much hiss.")

In 1972, Mitchell would pay the price for her unrepentant musical stance, when *Rolling Stone* dismissively termed her "Old Lady of the Year," visually depicting her as a lipstick kiss in the middle of a family tree of the Los Angeles music scene. Unsurprisingly, none of the men in the chart suffered this type of indignity (if anything, their inclusion in that graphic enhanced their clout).

"The patriarchy is a motherfucker," John Doe of X, The Blasters, and punk supergroup The Flesh Eaters states flatly about the sexism Mitchell faced — and faces still, in terms of her legacy. "I agree with her. I think that Neil Young and Bob Dylan and people that are her contemporaries get way more attention, more honor."

Matsson agrees. To him, Mitchell's legacy represents "a massive amount of fearlessness, and also being fearless of showing your weaknesses. It feels like the windows were blown open, and doing that in the middle of the patriarchy and not getting things for free — that probably all the other dudes in the '60s and the '70s got — to be considered rock stars and geniuses. And she just ... kept on trucking, kept on doing it."

What she also kept on doing was to continue to inspire both her contemporaries and new generations of artists. A concert celebrating Mitchell's 75th birthday last year featured Graham Nash and Kris Kristofferson, as well as Rufus Wainright and Norah Jones, culminating in a live tribute album released this past March. A recent photo of her walking through an art gallery with English visual artist David Hockney went viral on Instagram, garnering more than two million views.

In discussing the album, jazz/blues/gospel vocalist Lizz Wright noted that for her, "[*Clouds*] has to be the Joni record that I actually like to stand inside of the most."

Wright continues, "[Mitchell] just sits so deep in her humanity that I feel — especially as a woman of color with a big instrument and a lot of emotion — that I've been given a kind of blessing and permission and affirmation to be tender, and to stand flat-footed on the ground with no shoes and just be a poet." ∎

The Tallest Man on Earth

Music appreciation starts early at the Old Town School of Folk Music, with programs like Wiggleworms for babies and parents or caregivers.

TEACHING AND LEARNING

Folk music schools link the past, present, and future

by Bonnie Stiernberg

"I think sometimes there's a bit of nostalgia for 'this is what we've always done' that keeps us blind to what other kinds of things we could do that younger students could benefit from, be interested in, and maybe discover the Old Town School for."
Paul Tyler

WHEN CHICAGO'S legendary Old Town School of Folk Music first opened its doors more than 60 years ago, the folk music that founders Frank Hamilton, Win Stracke, and Dawn Greening sought to teach and promote occupied a far different space in pop culture than it does today.

"When it began in 1957, the definition of what folk music was was a slightly different thing, but it was a rediscovery of a part of American life that was in danger not of disappearing but of being buried by urban urges for everything to be new and modern and commodified," says Paul Tyler, an instructor at the Old Town School for more than 30 years. "And so the folk revival of the 1950s and '60s was, in a way, anti-modern. Not being backwards, but just to say, 'Hey, there's a whole lot of who we are that is just being completely forgotten or overlooked.' At that time, folk music was the kind of

thing that you kind of had to know what to do to go find it, and there were so many aspects of culture that were trying to tell you, 'Oh, that's not important, that's just rural people, that's just hicks, and they're not what life is about.'"

The school expanded as interest in folk music did, moving to larger locations to accommodate more classes in 1968 and again in 2012. The names of the artists who have graced its halls — as performers, instructors, students, or some combination of the three — reads like a who's who of the genre: Pete Seeger, Mahalia Jackson, Big Bill Broonzy, Steve Goodman, John Prine. Nowadays, it serves approximately 6,600 students a week, 2,700 of whom are children, and similar schools dedicated to teaching and preserving folk music's traditions have cropped up across the country.

Schools that teach folk traditions (including crafting, art, and other skills) are fairly common throughout the US, but few focus solely on music. Another

Eric D. Johnson of Fruit Bats

music-centric school is the Jalopy Theatre & School of Music in Brooklyn, New York's Red Hook neighborhood. Founded in 2006 by Lynette Wiley and her husband, Geoff, it serves as a community for local creatives and anyone interested in traditional folk music.

"We really realized the need for a facility for artists to gather is so important because collaboration can't happen when everybody's not coming together," Wiley explains. Jalopy features an elevated main stage in the middle of its 1,400 square-foot space. But more than just a performance venue, it encompasses a music school, an art gallery, an in-house record label called Jalopy Records, and an instrument shop where Geoff repairs and restores vintage gear. It's a place where people can gather, create, and find ways to support their art financially.

"It was really the musicians who helped us gain a reputation and who took a risk on playing a place as out of the way as we were at that time," she adds. "I mean, Brooklyn has changed a lot since then and our neighborhood has changed a lot, but when we started, this was the end of the earth."

Student-Teacher Bonds

The sense of camaraderie and dedication to fostering relationships between instructors and students is what sets most folk music schools apart from more traditional music programs.

"Students at the Old Town School, they're not there for a degree, they're not there for credits; it's recreational, community-based music," Tyler says. "They're there because they want to play. So it's very easy to relate to them as peers. I just think of it as a bunch of friends hanging out in a living room and playing. And I've got stuff to show them, and they come to my living room — though it's not my living room, it's the Old Town School — because they thought that I could teach them something."

It's that philosophy that appealed to Fruit Bats' Eric D. Johnson, who eventually became a banjo teacher at the Old Town School after starting out as a student and working an assortment of odd jobs there. "I even cleaned branches off the roof," he exclaims.

"I was teaching Beginning Banjo only like two years after I had learned myself," he says. "I think their idea was that somebody who was a good beginner

would be good at teaching complete beginners, which is cool. It's certainly not Juilliard. It is sort of about connection and connectivity, and for some reason they saw something in me that would be good at that."

Johnson, whose newest Fruit Bats record, *Gold Past Life*, will be released in June via Merge Records, is adamant that without those years teaching, his own music career would never have taken off the way it did.

"It was a really incredibly important experience for me and probably the place that launched my life in every way," he says. "Probably the most important thing from a professional or creative standpoint that ever happened to me was finding that pamphlet [advertising the school]."

The school is even the reason he wound up playing with experimental rock band Califone: A student of his was friends with the group and told him they were looking for someone "who could do folkie stuff but was kind of a weirdo."

"I ended up sort of blundering my way into a gig with those guys and then going on this massive tour with them, opening for Modest Mouse, and then I met The Shins on that tour," Johnson

A performance at the Old Town School of Folk Music in 1957 featuring Win Stracke and Frank Hamilton.

Jams abound at the Old Town School of Folk Music, including before and after classes as students pause to play together.

says. "Basically I got seamed in to the indie rock world single-handedly without having to do anything. It was just like one of my students kind of recommended me and then I just got dropped into a whole gigantic world, which is still the world I live in."

He also credits his time teaching at the Old Town School with helping him hone his own songwriting and performance skills.

"I really remember just a lot of teaching those group classes, which is the thing that taught me more than I could have imagined about how to be in a band and how to be a performer," he says. "It sounds cliché, but I was learning as much as I was teaching. It totally informed everything I do now. But it really had a lot to do with those nighttime group guitar classes because it was such a performance every night that you were doing: It was an energy transfer between people. It's sort of teaching people how to capture the energy of something. And it just sort of taught me a lot about how to make my own music."

Seemingly mundane tasks like making lead sheets with lyrics and chords for students made him look at songs in a different way, Johnson said, and talking about songs' meanings forced him to examine them up close,

too. "It made me realize what I liked and didn't like as a songwriter. It made me realize, 'I like this chord, I don't like this chord.' It was really like a biology course in music."

What Is Folk, Anyway?

According to Tyler at the Old Town School, folk music today doesn't have the same rigidity as it used to — either in terms of genre confines or the school's curriculum. "Now," he says, quick to laugh, "folk music is kind of 'Are you a person? Do you play music?'"

Both the Old Town School and Jalopy offer numerous workshops for kids and adults (Old Town School also has special lessons for teenagers and music classes for toddlers). Between the two schools, group instrumental offerings include accordion, banjo, bass, cello, drums, dulcimer, fiddle, guitar, harmonica, mandolin, piano, and ukulele. Plus, both offer private lessons, songwriting classes, and more.

Typically the repertoire, especially at the Old Town School, is broad but traditional, although the guitar program has a more nebulous definition of folk than other departments. The Old Town School even offers different styles of guitar lessons from different regions

around the world, when those niche teachers are available.

"Our songbook is traditional material because of publishing rights and stuff, but the guitar program supplements that with more popular material," Tyler explains. "There's a huge array of what's being offered there, so people can [learn] almost any kind of artists that they're familiar with from the pop music field. And I use 'pop music' in a very broad sense."

The definition of "folk" continues to evolve in terms of performances at both schools as well. Students are exposed to music from all over the world, often from artists whose music is a melting pot of influences. Sometimes, like with The Salaam-Shalom Project, a group that blends traditional Middle Eastern, South Asian, and Jewish sounds and recently performed at the Old Town School, the aim is to bridge cultural divides and foster goodwill through music. Other times, it's simply to rock the joint.

"We had an Arabic band as part of our World Music Wednesdays concert series a while back, and the place was rockin'. It was an electronic band playing Arabic rhythms, and the room was just — people were dancing, and the young people in there, the energy was just so hot. And those people are in Chicago! We should be able to find some that would be able to come and teach and help us open ourselves up to that kind of music community. Even though it's electronic, it's folk music."

Modern Challenges

Nowadays, younger students have access to all kinds of musical instruction at their fingertips thanks to the internet, and folk music schools are faced with the challenge of drawing in new generations who may not see the need for them.

Tyler notes that in his 30 years of teaching, the Old Town School has experienced growth for 28 years. In the past two years, it's seen a decline, possibly due to Chicago's population loss, neighborhood demographic changes, or technology. In particular, he sees the enrollment issues as stemming from two problems — difficulty appealing to younger generations and a lack of diversity.

"I think sometimes there's a bit of nostalgia for 'this is what we've always done' that keeps us blind to what other kinds of things we could do that younger students could benefit from, be interested in, and maybe discover the Old Town School for," he says.

"We have a lot to learn on how to become a fully multicultural place," Tyler continues. "We have to change the makeup of our faculty. When I look at the guitar program, it's very white. ... I think we need to broaden the ethnic diversity of our faculty and let them teach everything they can teach. We have a lot of integration to do in the true sense of the word. We need to really integrate our programs so that we look like what the city of Chicago looks like."

Diversity is a priority for Wiley as well. Jalopy puts on five festivals each year and the organization is eager to grow its international festival in particular.

"We're so proud of it," Wiley says. "We look into New York's ethnic communities, and we bring bands that are generally playing just for their communities together for a long weekend. And for many of them, this is the first time [for example] a Peruvian band has seen a band from Tibet. It's really exciting in what happens with the artists and with the audience to see such a broad array of music. And we feel like it's a real statement on the vibrancy of the New York immigrant community and that that's a really important place to put a focus these days, [along with] what we are all gaining and learning by their presence and by the music they all bring us, and so we'd love to see that festival grow."

That sort of expansion is key, and it's something Wiley says she's been able to pursue since Jalopy began operating as a nonprofit in 2017. She and her husband worked at Jalopy 110 hours a week for nine years before they had children and realized that model wasn't sustainable for anyone.

"Our hope has always been that we would be able to support artists in as many ways as possible, and first and foremost is a healthy organization to do that, and with the economies of scale in a city like New York, we frankly weren't going to be able to be here any longer if we didn't make the transition to a nonprofit," she says. "And so now that we are operating that way, we've been able to reach out to the community and friends and supporters have given us funding that has allowed us to strengthen the organization. We're raising teacher pay starting in June, so that artists will be making more that way. With the record label [Jalopy Records] we're hoping to receive some funding so that we can produce the first album of many more of the artists that play here. And then also a major goal for the next year and a half is to take these artists on the road and support them through tours and Jalopy Presents events around New York City [and] around the country as well, giving them the exposure and supporting their tours."

That all-hands-on-deck mentality has carried on throughout Jalopy's transition to a nonprofit, and it has resulted in an extremely tight-knit community. That strong sense of fellowship is integral to keeping folk music schools alive, and it's not something you can get online.

"There's something completely elemental about people singing together, and you can't get that on YouTube," Johnson says. "You're not singing with a group of people in a room. And honestly the sound of like 17 guitars playing at the same time is crazy and awesome, and you also don't get that on YouTube."

Tyler agrees, noting that the internet can be a great starting point, but places like the Old Town School are necessary to truly experience folk music.

"If people have some sort of quest that has been aided by YouTube or the internet or what have you, we can help them in a way that YouTube and the internet can't help them," he says. "We can put them together with real, living people who are doing the same thing they are and let them play together and let them experience music-making in the same room, human music-making as personal interaction. That's the strength of the Old Town School experience. Because you can go find someone to give you Skype lessons, and you might find the right teacher and really get advanced, but you're gonna miss that social interpersonal element."

Wiley agrees that the informal group settings of folk music schools offer the best way for students to learn.

"Playing in community brings people together," Wiley says. "It allows people to share. It makes connections between people and it opens them up. And when they're open, they can receive information and learn and care more. So we've always said with a very open and lighthearted style of learning, you'll advance as a musician and then we'll be able to teach you the history of these folk musicians whose music you'll be playing but also the stories of the people that the music is telling." ∎

Jalopy Theatre and School of Music

THERE IS POWER

The continuing history of labor songs

by Kim Kelly

Joe Hill

"Anyone can make a speech, but with a speech, you're just applauding what somebody's saying. When you come together and sing 'Solidarity Forever' or 'We Shall Overcome,' you are expressing your solidarity, your unity as a crowd."
Billy Bragg

There is power in a factory, power in the land,
Power in the hands of a worker.
But it all amounts to nothing if together we don't stand.
There is power in a union.

O GOES ONE OF THE MOST iconic songs in the labor movement's increasingly dusty canon. From the distorted clang of its opening chord through its rousing chorus — perfectly tailored for picket line sing-alongs — "There Is Power in a Union" immediately calls to mind mental images of sweaty men with hard hats and dirty faces, the groan of heavy machinery, and an honest day's work fighting the boss. It's a beloved staple, enshrined in the repertoire of any self-respecting lefty songbird, and much like its fellows — "Solidarity Forever," "Which Side Are You On?" "The Preacher and the Slave," "The Rebel Girl," etc. — the ditty boasts its own particular biography woven into the very

fabric of this nation.

And in some ways there may be nothing more American than the fact that one of the most cherished labor songs of the American left was originally composed by a Swedish immigrant, and then repurposed and popularized by a son of East London.

It's impossible to examine the history of American labor songs without the outsize legacy of Joe Hill. Born Joel Emmanuel Hägglund on the east coast of Sweden in 1879, he moved to the US in 1902, bouncing from New York City to Cleveland to San Francisco. He survived a catastrophic 1906 earthquake and in 1910 found employment as a dockworker. This is where his radical sensibilities first stirred, and when he joined the Industrial Workers of the

World (IWW), an anti-capitalist, equality-minded international labor union also known as Wobblies.

It was under their banner that he began writing and composing songs for use in inciting, inspiring, and organizing workers, many of which found inclusion in the organization's *Little Red Songbook*, a regularly issued compendium of rabble-rousing odes meant to be sung around campfires and at protests. Later compiled into the *Big Red Songbook* (with a foreword by longtime Wobbly and labor advocate Tom Morello of Rage Against the Machine), Hill's best-known songs typically swiped melodies from popular songs and hymns for maximum impact, and include the aforementioned "The Rebel Girl" and "There Is Power in a Union" as well as the jaunty "The Preacher and the Slave," "The Tramp," and "Casey Jones — the Union Scab."

Hill's songs have surfaced in a variety of pop cultural and musical contexts throughout the years, some more unexpected than others. For example, Philadelphia folk punks Mischief Brew's rip-roaring rendition of "The Preacher and the Slave" relies heavily on banjo and late vocalist Erik Petersen's scratchy yowl, while labor organizer and folkie Utah Phillips stuck

to a more straightforward approach.

Farther north, Boston punks Street Dogs tackled "There Is Power in a Union," as did oddball folk rockers The Mountain Goats and, perhaps most famously, British singer, songwriter, and activist Billy Bragg, whose arrangement and retooling of Hill's version has become more popular — or at the very least, far better known — than the original.

Bragg traces his political awakening back to his first Rock Against Racism concert in 1978, which led to his fervent support of striking British coal miners during their brutal 1984 battle with UK Prime Minister Margaret Thatcher and served as a springboard for a lifetime of activism. By now, Bragg's name is synonymous with political music, and his cover of classic labor songs in particular have shown remarkable staying power. His version of "There Is Power in a Union" has become iconic in and of itself, and the passion woven into every line stems from his experiences singing for those striking miners.

"The first time I did a gig up in the coalfield, the guy who was opening for me was an old miner, and he sat onstage with his hand over his ear and he sang a cappella songs — and all of his songs

were more radical than mine!" Bragg remembers. "And I stood in the wings thinking, 'Shit, what am I gonna do now?' And I joked with him about it when he came offstage, and he said, 'Son, it doesn't matter what you sing out there, the fact that you're standing up for the miners, you're part of this tradition.' I've always thought that's a really important sense of how you become part of something — being there, expressing your solidarity. The songs are the glue that hold that together."

The Rebel Girls

While Hill was undeniably one of the most influential songwriters in labor history, he wasn't the only one worth celebrating. Women's voices have not always been lifted as high as they should have been in the context of pro-labor songs, but they are behind some of its most enduring anthems. "Which Side Are You On?", written by labor activist and coal miner's wife Florence Reece, lies very much in the same vein, and has been interpreted by a host of old-school folk singers as well as black metal band Panopticon, rapper Talib Kweli, Boston punks Dropkick Murphys, songwriter

Ani DiFranco, and hip-hop outfit Rebel Diaz (with an assist from Dead Prez).

Reece wrote the song at her kitchen table, scrawling her words on an old calendar as her husband, an organizer for the United Mine Workers, who were then locked in a bloody fight with coal mine operators called the Harlan County War, slept in the next room, worn out from the picket lines and from tussling with the bosses' hired goons. She lifted the melody from the traditional folk ballad "Jack Monroe," which itself mirrored a Baptist hymn; she, like Hill, understood the power of simple, memorable melodies and powerful words. Reece took no prisoners, spelling out the struggle in plain language and calling out Sheriff J.H. Blair, who aided and abetted the bosses' terror campaign against the miners and their families:

They say in Harlan County,
There are no neutrals there.
You'll either be a union man
Or a thug for J. H. Blair.
Which side are you on boys?
Which side are you on?

The song was popularized by seminal bluegrass singer and bandleader Hazel Dickens, who was herself a staunch feminist and union supporter who wrote many songs about the harsh realities of Appalachian life and in support of striking coal miners. A coal miner's daughter-turned-factory worker, Dickens appeared in the landmark Mine Wars documentary *Harlan County USA* alongside Reece and contributed four songs to its soundtrack, her reedy, soaring twang extolling the virtues of hardworking union men and raining scorn upon the crooked bosses whose greedy machinations cut so many lives short. Her rendition of "The Rebel Girl" loops back to Joe Hill, but imbues the song with a gritty, personal pathos that could only have sprung from the lips of a real-life rebel girl.

Her song "Fire in the Hole" in particular remains one of the most defiant odes to working class rebellion that the American labor movement has ever heard, its spare, uncompromising lyrics laying bare the fire that burned in those hills, its very title a warning: "Oh, daddy died a miner and grandpa, he did too / I'll bet this coal will kill me 'fore my working days is through / When a hole is dark and dirty, an early grave you'll find / I plan to make a union for the ones I leave behind."

Much more recently, the feminist labor anthem "Bread and Roses" was given a millennial boost thanks to its inclusion in a pivotal scene in the 2014 film *Pride*, which told the story of a group of gay and lesbian activists in London who raised money for the families of Welsh miners impacted by the miners' strike of 1984. Originally written as a poem by James Oppenheim and set to music by Caroline Kohlsaat in 1917, the song has become a rallying cry for a worker's right to not only live, but to live a decent life — to have bread in their cupboards and roses upon their table.

As we go marching, marching,
unnumbered women dead
Go crying through our singing their
ancient song of bread
Small art and love and beauty their
drudging spirits knew
Yes, it is bread we fight for —
but we fight for roses, too!

Labor leader Rose Schneiderman is credited with coining the phrase itself, and it became a symbol of the 1912 textile strike in Lawrence, Massachusetts — also known as the Bread and Roses strike. It was resurrected by activist and songwriter Mimi Fariña, who reset it to music in 1974, and whose older sister, Joan Baez, performed a popular cover (Fariña's version of the song was also recorded by Judy Collins, Ani DiFranco, Utah Phillips, and John Denver). It also inspired the name of now-defunct Boston folk punk outfit Bread and Roses, who peppered their upbeat acoustic ditties with pro-labor slogans and tales of adventure and, unsurprisingly, covered Billy Bragg as well.

Picket Lines and Politics

Mainstream music is more political than ever, but specifically union-focused songs have largely disappeared from the airwaves in favor of a broader social consciousness. However, as far as Bragg

Son Volt

can make out, the causes of dissent may have shifted, but the classic songs that modern radicals reach for in times of crisis and solidarity often remain constant — and we ignore their power at our own peril.

"The picket lines have changed, maybe; the ones I've been on lately have been around climate change," he says. "The students close by where I live had a day-long picket at Exeter University, and they invited me along. Before I went, I spoke to the guy and said, 'Sure, I'll come down, but just can you tell me songs you're singing on the picket line, because I want to be able to plug into what you're doing.' And they were singing 'Solidarity Forever' and 'There Is Power in a Union.' Now, 'Solidarity Forever' is more synonymous with the American struggle, but as far as they was concerned, that was the song for their strike, because solidarity is solidarity wherever you go."

The spirit of those old songs remains firm, but despite a recent resurgence in labor power and an uptick in positive public perception of unions overall, today's socially conscious artists are looking beyond the shop floor and the union hall for inspiration.

"I think it might be that the culture has changed in a significant way," Bragg muses. "It's not easy to sing [Childish Gambino's] 'This Is America' on a picket line, despite the fact that it's an incredibly powerful song, it's an incredibly political song, and all of us understand what it's saying. But it's not something that's easily reproduced by a bunch of people standing around in the cold. It's the nature of those songs, and I think Joe Hill understood this, because he only wrote lyrics. He took the tunes of popular songs, and hymns that everybody knew, and he wrote the lyrics to fit those tunes, because people would already know the tune. He wasn't starting from scratch, so he was

plugging into his contemporary culture, in the same way that Woodie [Guthrie] did, and the same way that I did. I was fortunate in that I was making those songs at a time when the idea of music as a vehicle for change in the world was still current."

Folk music has always provided welcome quarter for labor activists and union men and maids, and there's still much to be said for the power of three chords and the truth — whether those chords are rendered on acoustic strings, plucked on steel guitar, or come layered with distortion. Midwestern alt-country quintet Son Volt drew on all three when it came time to craft their own entry into the canon, and while their sound leans most heavily toward lonesome acoustics and barroom rock, you can tell they've thought about Joe Hill once or twice, too.

"Both folk music and punk rock were havens for political content and I was influenced by both early on," Son Volt vocalist and multi-instrumentalist Jay

Farrar explains via email. On the alt-country outfit's latest release, which came out in March and is aptly titled *Union*, Farrar and his compatriots made their allegiances clear. Of particular note is their cover of Joe Hill's classic "The Rebel Girl," which was originally written in 1915 in honor of Elizabeth Gurley Flynn, a fire-breathing orator and organizer for the IWW who once chained herself to a lamppost during a violent protest in Spokane, Washington, and refused to back down when the cops came in swinging. Farrar hadn't heard the original before recording Son Volt's version, but found himself captivated by the lyrics, inadvertently falling under the spell of century-old Wobbly propaganda in the process.

The rebel girl he and Hill sing of is a proud freedom fighter, a "precious pearl" in a ragged dress whose hands are hardened from labor, but whose bosom swells with revolutionary zeal. In Farrar's version, lush acoustic guitars offer a simple accompaniment to Hill's impassioned words, delivered in a husky, world-weary twang that wouldn't sound out of place in one of the Pacific Northwestern lumber camps where the IWW laid down roots and the original Rebel Girl traveled to spread the gospel of working class liberation. It's a

beautiful piece of continuity, and given how much of Hill's vast catalog has been neglected and lain fallow, it's a thrill to hear this song resurrected by a contemporary artist.

Son Volt also channeled two of labor's most revered figures during the recording of Union, the iconic labor organizer Mary "Mother Jones" Harris and folk singer Woodie Guthrie. Songs like "The 99" and "The Symbol" were recorded at the Mother Jones Museum in Mt. Olive, Illinois, and the Woody Guthrie Center in Tulsa, Oklahoma, "to both highlight their contributions and to hopefully inspire this project along the way by paying homage to those folks that made a difference," Farrar explains. Album closer "The Symbol" was also directly inspired by Guthrie's "Deportee (Plane Wreck at Los Gatos)" and binds the threads of history even tighter.

A final, yet critical entry in the larger canon of labor songs that connects past, present, and future is "We Shall Overcome." Bragg cites it in particular for both its versatility in addressing different, yet interconnected struggles and its added purpose of reminding listeners what an integral role black civil rights leaders played in the American labor movement. The most

recognizable modern version of the song first appeared in 1945 during a cigar workers strike made up primarily of black women and led by Lucille Simmons — who is credited with changing the original lyric from "I" to "we," tapping into that collective solidarity that Bragg describes.

"You've got to find a way of connecting with the struggle, and the places where you need those songs now are places like the Women's March, or in Ferguson, in that context, where people are stood together confronting the police. A song can send a message," Bragg says. "That has persisted despite changes in culture. You need something that expresses the unity of everyone who's come together. Anyone can make a speech, but with a speech, you're just applauding what somebody's saying. When you come together and sing 'Solidarity Forever' or 'We Shall Overcome,' you are expressing your solidarity, your unity as a crowd."

He continues, "You can't just knock those songs off. They come with a great sense of tradition, and by singing them in that context, you're reaching out to that tradition and drawing power from that struggle — the idea that people have fought before, and won before, and that we're going to win this one again." ∎

Billy Bragg

Honoring Pete Seeger

Pete Seeger would have turned 100 years old on May 3, 2019. As a songwriter, collector, interpreter, instrumentalist, and activist, Seeger inspired generations of musicians and fans with his decades of work. A tireless advocate with an insatiable curiosity, he never stopped peacefully assembling for social justice or seeking music that would help such causes.

Here at *No Depression*, we often theme entire issues on certain musical genres. So for this issue about folk music, it seemed fitting to honor Seeger and his lifelong dedication to the form, its stories, and its people. In the following pages, we explore lesser-told sides of Seeger's musical career, including how his popularization of "We Shall Overcome" encapsulates the larger folk process, his local legacy in his beloved Hudson River Valley, and modern parallels to the blacklisting and censorship he experienced and, indeed, overcame.

— *Hilary Saunders*

CHANGING WITH THE TIMES

The folk process keeps freedom songs alive across generations

by Kim Ruehl

African American and white supporters of the Mississippi Freedom Democratic Party hold signs in front of the convention hall at the 1964 Democratic National Convention, Atlantic City, New Jersey.

ONE RAINY DAY IN THE autumn of 1945, as time marched toward a new year and the temperature along the coast of South Carolina plummeted low enough to threaten snow, a young black woman named Lucille Simmons stood out in the weather and sang a verse:

We will overcome
We will overcome
We will overcome someday ...

Simmons was a member of the Congress of Industrial Organizations' Food, Tobacco, Agricultural and Allied Workers Union, or FTA-CIO. She and her colleagues at Charleston's American Tobacco factory were on strike to demand a fairer wage and an integrated factory floor. For five months — day in and day out, from six in the morning until six at night — one thousand members of the American Tobacco's FTA-CIO, black and white alike, were on strike. And every day, before anyone headed home, Simmons insisted they sing this song with her.

The melody was at least centuries old: It can be heard in the Catholic hymn "O Sanctissima," which dates back to 17th century Europe. At some point the melody migrated to the United States, where it bounced around mostly undocumented from unrecorded community to unrecorded community.

Then, in 1900, a composer named Charles Tindley published a hymn called "I'll Overcome Someday." Although some scholars have credited Tindley, a white man, with creating the song that eventually became the anthem of the civil rights movement (and while the lyrics employ similar verbiage), it's easy to hear that the melody of Tindley's composition does not match that of the freedom song. Rather, a closer parallel might be the early 1930s composition "If My Jesus Wills," written by Louise Shropshire of Cincinnati, Ohio.

Shropshire was born a sharecropper, but her family soon moved north in search of a better life. As an adult, she was active in her church choir and wrote a number of gospel songs for them to sing, many of which began to circulate throughout other black churches in the East and South. Though it's hard to be certain, many presume that "If My Jesus Wills" had become a standard at the Baptist church in Charleston, South Carolina, where Lucille Simmons sang in the choir.

Shropshire's song slowed down the "O Sanctissima" melody, adding a gospel swing to it and pulling together lyrics of transcendence that echoed those composed by Tindley. Whether she was cobbling together elements from various known source materials or whether her songwriting process was more spiritual and nuanced is unknown. But what is abundantly clear is that the song Shropshire published was an antecedent to the song that would become so pervasive in American movements that it would eventually be quoted by President Lyndon B. Johnson during a joint session of Congress.

What is perhaps most fascinating about "We Shall Overcome" — though it is by no means exclusive to that song — is the way this centuries-old melody coalesces with the timeless theme of striving to surmount oppression. It has woven itself into a completely new song over the course of several generations

Highlander Folk School Music Director Zilphia Horton leads singing on a picket line in Chattanooga, Tennessee, in the late 1930s.

on American soil.

Many folk musicians are familiar with this type of musical evolution, and have coined a phrase to explain it: the folk process.

The folk process is the method by which a song grows and evolves over the course of time due to the contributions of people who are separated often by generations, regions, and races, and occasionally ideologies. The best folk songs, those that prove universally applicable, meander through communities, connecting all those who sing them in something of a musical chain across time.

No Direct Path

In an attempt to present the convoluted evolution of "We Shall Overcome," Pete Seeger once tried to list everything he knew about the song during a 2006 interview with Tim Robbins for Pacifica Radio. Seeger didn't seem to know about

Shropshire at the time, but he was aware of many other outcroppings of the song across history. Though the dates he quoted were not correct, his approximation offered a pretty good view of the way the folk process moves a song from one place to another, changing it as it goes.

"Most of us thought it had been put together in 1946, because that's when the slow version of it was put together by tobacco workers," Seeger said. "They'd say, 'Here comes Lucille. Now we'll hear that song sung slower than anybody's [sung it].'

"About four years ago, I'm sent a book called *The Challenge of Interracial Unionism* by a professor in the University of Pennsylvania. And there was a Xeroxed copy of a letter in the United Mine Workers journal of February 1909 and the letter on the front page says ... 'We started every meeting with a prayer and singing that good old song, "We Will Overcome."' ... Whether they sang it fast or whether

they slowed it down, I don't know. The newspaper article didn't say. But in 1946, Lucille Simmons must have remembered it and slowed it down.

"Zilphia Horton, who was a white union organizer, the wife of Myles Horton, she had a beautiful alto voice and she learned the song from the tobacco workers and taught it to me."

Seeger had met Horton in 1940 when he went on a road trip through the South with Woody Guthrie and the pair spent a couple of days at Horton's home, at the Highlander Folk School in Tennessee. In the years since, he had started a magazine called *People's Songs* out of his house in New York. In the autumn of 1948, Seeger printed Horton's version of "We Will Overcome" in *People's Songs*, putting it in 4/4 time and adding the instruction, "Sing it very slowly and freely the way Zilphia picked it up."

"I tried to sing it with a banjo accompaniment," he told Robbins, "but it never went anywhere, until 1960."

The best folk songs, those that prove universally applicable, meander through communities, connecting all those who sing them in something of a musical chain across time.

Five years after Rosa Parks thrust the civil rights struggle into the national consciousness when she refused to yield her seat on a Montgomery, Alabama, bus, the civil rights movement was making nationwide headlines. Horton had died and a folksinger from California named Guy Carawan had taken her place at Highlander. Seeger recalled that, in the spring of 1960, Carawan "invited about 70 young people for a workshop at Highlander. ... They had a whole weekend called, 'Singing in the Movement' — slow songs, fast songs, serious songs, sad songs, funny songs. The hit of the weekend was 'We Shall Overcome,' but Guy was singing it the way we know it now. He gave it a strong, pulsing rhythm.

"Five weeks later in Raleigh, North Carolina, Guy is at the founding convention of SNCC [Student Nonviolent Coordinating Committee]. And somebody shouts from the audience, 'Guy, teach us all We Shall Overcome,' so this white man from California [was] singing this song from African Americans. ... Three years later I'm up in Carnegie Hall and gave it that strong pulse with the bass. Pretty

soon the audience was singing it. That's the only record of mine that ever sold in any quantity."

It's notable that not even Seeger, an exquisite storyteller and lifelong collector of songs, was able to create a straight line on the narrative of this traditional song. The folk process is often meandering and nonsensical, and often less important to understand than the song it delivers to the people who need it, when they need it.

For example, we know people throughout history have seen fit to express the need to surmount oppression and struggle through music. We know that this particular song came together thanks to a belief shared across centuries: If we work together and organize together, we will overcome. We know a few pinpointable historical benchmarks, like the story of Lucille Simmons and American Tobacco. We know that when Zilphia Horton wrote an introduction to the song in the 1948 issue of *People's Songs*, she applauded the fact that "(i)ts strong emotional appeal and simple dignity never fails to hit people. It sort of stops them cold silent."

With that, she was referring not to the

work that she put into the song. After Horton learned it from Simmons' colleagues in the FTA-CIO, the three verses she nailed down and passed on to Seeger were anything but an exercise in ego, nor an expression of any single songwriter. Rather, she was invoking the human heart of the song, the spirit of it that persisted no matter what group of people decided to take it up and sing it, no matter where they were and what they were for or against. She crafted it specifically for the folk process to give it wings.

As it turned out, people found it arresting. They felt compelled to sing it. They still do, and the song continues to grow and change. The folk process is eternal.

Giving Credit

There is considerably more to the story of "We Shall Overcome" than can be contained in this article. Several books have been written in an attempt to trace its story and *No Depression* even published another article specifically about it in the Fall 2016, *Speak Up!* issue. It remains a popular topic to explore, and a fresh one, because it exemplifies how songs emerge and shift and change through the number of people who touch them, the various contexts in which they're sung, the tangents and conflicting narratives of origination, and more.

To those who are accustomed to music as something that has a clear author, it may seem necessary to pinpoint singular authorship in order to give credit where it's due; however, this notion is a result of the commodification of music over the past century. It doesn't have any real standing in the way music actually lives in the world, especially the songs typically categorized as folk songs.

When it comes to commercialized folk music, few songwriters have explored the folk process more consistently and artistically than Bob Dylan, who runs his own original songs through the process from performance to performance and recording to recording. It's Dylan's willingness to process his own compositions that often makes his audiences anxious, and yet, he's drawing from the way he learned about music in the first place — by listening to folk songs. (In Jonathan Cott's book *Dylan on Dylan*, the songwriter noted that his songs "float in a luminous haze," and that, perhaps most notably, "You don't write a song to sit there on the page. You write it to sing it.")

His hero Woody Guthrie — a contemporary of Seeger, Horton, and Simmons — did this too, often tossing in verses on the fly. Guthrie's most famous composition, "This Land Is Your Land," was rammed through the folk process for a time when a verse about private property was removed for being too provocative. Folksingers have long since asserted the process back on the song, resurrecting the lost verse thanks in no small part to Guthrie's son Arlo, who always performs the song in full. Occasionally protesters pull the song out at rallies and have been known to add new verses to apply to the present situation.

The reality of our most enduring folk songs is that the process is what grants them staying power. It is their ability to evolve, to be employed in any situation, to link people together across time and various differences, that gives them value. Because of the way these songs change, we can learn about the way society has changed. We can see our ability to evolve reflected in their ongoing evolutions.

Fans of recorded music tend to seek the version of a song that first moved them, whereas folksingers and folk fans tend to seek the right song for the moment. If it doesn't fit exactly, they'll change it until it does.

Going Digital

The last few years of amplified activism — marches, sit-ins, rallies, and other organizing events — have spotlighted a return to mainstream consciousness of many of the songs that were brought to the fore decades ago by folks like Horton, Seeger, Carawan, and the SNCC Freedom Singers. Student activists are singing for gun control, changing verses and adding lyrics in the way that the folk process has handed these songs down: "Enough is enough today / Deep in my heart, I do believe we shall overcome someday."

We've seen people gathering at airports to protest a Muslim travel ban by singing "This Little Light of Mine." "This Land Is Your Land" is showing up again, as is "We Shall Not Be Moved" and even occasionally "Solidarity Forever."

But we can also see the folk process at work on more contemporary folk songs.

Take for example a composition by Wisconsin-based singer-songwriter Peter Mulvey, who challenged his fellow folksingers to record their own versions of a song he wrote called "Take Down Your Flag."

Two days after a white man shot nine black people in a church in Charleston, South Carolina, in 2015, Mulvey sat down to write a song that honored the victims even as it addressed the persistence of the Confederate flag.

Every flag in Charleston
is at half-mast today except one
You know which one
Take down your flag to half-mast ...
And then take it down for good.

Mulvey's second verse was a tribute to one of the victims, Susie Jackson, and when he posted the song online, a commenter asked why he only wrote a verse for one of the victims. Where were the other eight verses?

Inspired, Mulvey started challenging his folksinger friends to record the song, adding their own verses to honor those who were killed. He hoped this would result in eight new verses, but instead he watched close to 200 versions show up on social media.

Over the course of just a couple of months, versions appeared on YouTube by Keb' Mo', Peter Yarrow, Ani DiFranco, Vance Gilbert, Anaïs Mitchell, Pamela Means, The Steel Wheels, Amy Speace, Wild Ponies' Telisha Williams, Mark Erelli, and many more. Each verse follows the basic template set forth by Mulvey, but veers slightly in the way the performing songwriter crafted the verse

they added. Essentially, the song was completed by community consensus, a collective message created over a fairly short period of time, moving through the folk process in an acutely observable way.

While so many of the freedom songs we hear at marches and gatherings these days have evolved more like "We Shall Overcome" — over the course of centuries, passed from person to person, from community to community, from one equality-centered goal to another — Mulvey's folk process took a matter of months. But the effect was the same. The song stopped being about what Mulvey originally wanted to say and took on a life and meaning of its own, with Vance Gilbert even writing a verse about the shooter, challenging his (and our) ability to empathize.

Mulvey was delighted with the life his song took on, and acknowledges that the verses other people created brought something to the song that he never could have created on his own. In fact, he's made a habit of incorporating some of the other verses into his own performances of the song.

Peter Mulvey

"There's one verse in particular," he says. "I combined Mick McAuley's verse, 'Nine of our sisters and brothers are dead; let us bow down our heads to their names,' with Dinty Child's verse, 'Tywanza, Sharonda, Clementa, Cynthia, Ethel, Myra, Susie, Daniel, Depayne.' They rhyme by coincidence, and they make a powerful verse."

Further, Mulvey notes, deliberately sending a song out to be worked through the folk process has taught him a thing or two about the utility of music, and the possibilities of songwriting. "All songs, once written, no longer belong to the writer," he says. "But when a song gets 200 different rewrites of the second verse, as 'Take Down Your Flag' did, it makes that point so obviously that even I understood it."

Mulvey's point about songs not belonging to the writer brings us back to "We Shall Overcome," which was moved into the public domain after a court case that was decided last year. Seeger had paid for the copyright — attributing it to Horton, Carawan, Hamilton, and himself — to ensure that the song wasn't co-opted by commercial advertisers. The copyright also ensured that any proceeds from the song's sales went to a We Shall Overcome Fund maintained by the Highlander Research and Education Center, which directed the money to black-led organizations around the South. But the court case cited the folk process in the creation of the song, which wrested the verses from their copyright and placed the anthem in the public domain.

There's no way to know how this might affect the song's ongoing evolution. Though it will undoubtably impact the We Shall Overcome Fund, the copyright had never stopped organizers from calling it out during a rally to get the crowd singing along, just as Mulvey's copyright ownership on "Take Down Your Flag" won't stop folksingers from recording new versions and pumping the song ever further through the process.

Calling to mind an image in another song from Horton's collection, "We Shall Not Be Moved," these songs are like trees by the water — stretching out, changing shape, being blown by the wind and always growing in new directions. As long as we continue to honor them, feed them, give them room to grow, they will be there to offer shade and respite for generations to come. ■

HOMETOWN HERO

Pete Seeger's local legacy in the Hudson Valley

by Anne Margaret Daniel

SPRING CAME TO NEW YORK'S Hudson River Valley slowly this year. Despite the breaker boats keeping the shipping channel clear, thick slabs and floes remain on the edges of the Hudson until as late as May some years. The Hudson freezes even though it is tidal and brackish, churning and mixing freshwater from the Catskill creeks with the salt waters of Upper Bay for more than 150 miles, up past Albany, and well past the little town of Beacon. Pete and Toshi Ohta Seeger made their home just south of Beacon — at first camping out on the land, and then in a house that offered a view of the mighty Hudson River and was heated by wood stoves and, later on, powered by solar panels — from 1949 for the rest of their lives.

Pete and Toshi were both New Yorkers to the core. Seeger's mother, Constance, was a violinist who performed around the world and his father Charles was a musicologist, composer, and scholar of American music. Both taught at the Institute of Musical Art in New York City, which later became Juilliard. Toshi, born in Munich, moved to the city as a child and went to the Little Red Schoolhouse in Greenwich Village, spending summers and weekends in Woodstock. Her father, Takashi Ohta, was a designer for the Woodstock Playhouse and a writer; his 1929 memoir *The Golden Wind*, written with Margaret Sperry, is a wrenching story based in his own voluntary exile from a Japanese noble family. Toshi's mother, a Southern belle named Virginia Harper Berry, performed with the

Provincetown Players before her marriage to Ohta. From both of them, Toshi learned how to write, to shape an event, to set a stage. She and Pete met at a square dance in 1939, and were married for 70 years. They raised three children on the river bluffs in Beacon, but their joint legacy stretches the length of the Hudson Valley and beyond.

Ed Renehan, writer, publisher, musician, and close friend of the Seegers since the late 1960s, says, "They had decided to move out of the city and had about $700, borrowed, I think, from Pete's dad. [Pete] was born in Patterson, New York, so he had some connection to the Hudson Valley already, and they started looking there. A realtor showed them seven acres for sale at $100 an acre."

It was mostly steep hillside running

down to the 9D, a thin highway parallel to the river, and just a bit to the north of high land bearing the name Breakneck Ridge. Continues Renehan, "Pete started climbing up the mountainside, while Toshi stayed at the roadside with the realtor. He finally found an acre and a half that was flat."

On that acre and a half, the Seegers began to homestead. "He managed to get an old trailer up there, and he'd go and spend nights," continued Renehan. "When he had a day or so free, he'd catch the train and then hitchhike or walk from Beacon or Cold Spring and work on a two-room cabin. Some weekends they'd have work parties, like a barn raising."

The little cabin looked out on the Hudson, though the Seegers didn't know that, at first. Renehan recalls, "They didn't really realize the wonderful view, until Pete started chopping down trees. That really turned him on to the river." Today, the cabin is just one of the residences on the Seeger property, a guest house for those visiting Pete and Toshi's youngest daughter Tinya and her family.

It is impossible to speak of the Seegers' importance in the Hudson Valley in musical terms alone, for they were people who did their utmost to turn one of America's most polluted rivers back into a viable ecosystem again. When asked what Pete and Toshi taught him about matters other than music, Mike Merenda of the folk duo The Mammals says simply, "It's being a steward of the place where we live ... keeping an eye, and an ear, on things."

The River and a Project

It took a trip to Provincetown, Massachusetts, and a chance encounter with a man and a boat to send Seeger out onto the water, despite his decades of performing and recording various sea chanteys. "Pete didn't get into sailing until the late '50s or early '60s," says Renehan. "He was playing a concert in Provincetown, and Lillian Hellman had a party for him. At the party, a young man asked him if he'd like to go out on a sailboat, and Pete got the sailing bug. When he got back, within a year or two he bought himself a little used sailboat, a little Bristol or something, and kept it on the Hudson. That's when he became environmentally aware of the river."

Immediately upon this awareness, Seeger began to act. And when Seeger acted, results always followed. An early fundraising letter, on custom-printed "Hudson River Sloop Restoration Inc." stationery, is included in the more-than- 200-page book for the recently released six-disc set *Pete Seeger: The Smithsonian Collection.*

Pete knew how to deploy a "your" instead of "our." He wrote, "A Hudson River Sloop will sail from Maine to New York Harbor next summer and start its historic journey on our beloved Hudson if you support your project at this time."

Pete and Toshi first announced in 1966 their plan to "build a boat to save the river." In September 1968, Pete attended a meeting of the Mid-Hudson Intercounty Council and outlined the idea for what would be, literally, that flagship. The boat's plans had already been drawn, based upon the wooden packet boats that had plied the river's waters from its mouth to the fall line at the port of Albany in the days before steam. It was to be built in Maine, and then sailed to New York to spend its life sailing up and down the Hudson, for Seeger wished for the boat to be a constant reminder of past, present, and future — as he once described, "to recall the past of the communities that line the river and to make the citizens of them more aware of their historic heritage."

Exactly a year after Seeger's initial proposal to that council meeting, the local Kingston newspaper, *Daily Freeman*, was

Pete Seeger in June 1969

already praising Pete and the ship's multitalented crew, the Sloop Singers, for their anti-pollution efforts. Some local industrialists, and the politicians they supported, hated Seeger's project, but local churches and musicians and just about everyone else applauded.

To this day, the single-mast, gaff-rigged sloop Clearwater — 106 feet long and built at the Harvey Gamage Shipyard in South Bristol, Maine, for a total of $160,000 — still sails the Hudson as soon as the last of winter's ice has gone. Traffic on Manhattan's West Side Highway, and joggers in Riverside Park, slow to watch it as it makes its wide, leisurely way up and down, its shallow hull and three-thousand-plus feet of sail carrying the teaching ship and its passengers through every iteration of the river's shifting tides.

Personal Connections

Happy Traum, now 80, knows the exact moment when he began his own long, successful life as a musician: Friday, April 13, 1956. That day, some friends convinced Traum to trek from his home in the Bronx to hear Seeger at the Brooklyn Academy of Music in a benefit concert for school scholarships.

"I was 15 or 16 and didn't play the guitar at all. And I went to a Pete Seeger show in Brooklyn," Traum recalls. He describes the gig as just "one guy with an instrument, 1,500 people, and songs that were meaningful — songs that said something to me. It threw my whole world into wonder."

A decade later, Happy and his wife, Jane, followed the Seegers' footsteps upriver and moved from New York City to Woodstock, where they have taught and shared roots music via their Homespun Tapes, now Homespun Music Instruction, for more than 50 years.

The mid-Hudson Valley area has been regarded as salubrious and sacred since the days when the Esopus tribe, the branch of the Lenape nation living there when Dutch settlers first arrived, made it their home. From the early 1800s, visitors came to the area to paint it, thanks to Thomas Cole's pioneering Hudson Valley canvases, and for their health. Other artists, and musicians, followed. Twenty years after Seeger moved to Beacon, Albert Grossman, who had lived just west of Woodstock in Bearsville since the early 1960s, opened the Bearsville Recording Studio. The music manager's most celebrated client, Bob Dylan, moved to the area, too, and he and his wife, Sara, raised their growing family there until, in Dylan's

own words from his autobiography, *Chronicles, Volume One*, "rogue radicals looking for the Prince of Protest began to arrive — unaccountable-looking characters, gargoyle-looking gals, scarecrows, stragglers looking to party, raid the pantry." The Dylans decamped, though he returns to the area with some regularity. His American concert schedules usually sweep through upstate, and in 2017 included two dates at the old Hutton Brickyards in Kingston, New York, with concertgoers on the Hudson sailing up almost to the edge of backstage.

Multi-instrumentalist Jay Ungar, like Traum a Bronx-born boy and early performer in the Greenwich Village music scene of the early 1960s, also chose to make his home up the river. He and his first wife, Lyn Hardy, collaborated on pride-of-place records and tunes named for where they were, like Putnam County and the Catskill Mountains. Later, with his second wife, Molly Mason, Ungar would become the guiding hand and spirit of one of the most special places along a river laden with them, the Ashokan Center.

Ungar has said that Woodstock historian Alf Evers once told him "Ashokan" was a 17th-century Dutch corruption of the Lenape word meaning

Summer Hoot 2013 on the Toshi Stage. From left, Jay Ungar, Molly Mason, Mike Merenda, Pete Seeger, Will Merenda, Ruth Ungar

"a good place to fish." From 1912 to 1915, this was particularly relevant. The Ashokan Reservoir was constructed, drowning the little town and surrounding farms to form a snaking deep trench of more than 100 billion gallons of water for the use of the New York City Board of Water Supply. *The Poughkeepsie Eagle-News* reported in 1910 that New York City was sending "thousands of books from its public library ... for the benefit the laborers" at work on the reservoir and its dams and bridges — and that 2,800 graves had to be removed before work could even begin. Not everything precious in the area was submerged: A 1780s farmhouse built by a family called Winchell, the original schoolhouse for the hamlet of Marbletown, and a late 19th-century covered bridge all became part of New York's first outdoor environmental education organization, The Ashokan Field Campus. The 385-acre campus opened to schoolchildren in 1967 and now operates its outdoor programs

and much else under the name of the Ashokan Center.

Since 1981, Ungar has been running the Ashokan Fiddle & Dance Camps at the Center. These have spread and deepened into musical camps of all varieties. Next year will see bluegrass, acoustic guitar, klezmer, and autoharp and dulcimer camps; swing and western dancing camps and evenings; an all-star ukulele concert over Memorial Day weekend; and Summer and Winter Hoot events organized by Ungar's daughter Ruth and her husband, Mike Merenda, since 2013.

Ruth first met the Seegers when she was a child, at the Clearwater Festival. Since 1966, when those fundraising letters began, the Seegers organized a summer music event for the environmental support of, and in celebration of, the Hudson. "Dad booked the dance stage under Toshi," Ungar remembers. Twenty years later, she and Merenda would form their folk-rock band, The Mammals, with Seeger's

grandson Tao Rodríguez-Seeger. Rodríguez-Seeger had been performing with his grandfather since 1986, and Pete attended The Mammals' early shows. Ungar remembers Seeger playing with them in Great Barrington and some small local venues, but their first big performance with him was in 2002, at the Winter Olympic Games in Salt Lake City.

"Picture this: Tao, Mike, and me, working with local musicians and hundreds of children, and Pete," Ungar says. The children, working with a dance company, had learned their choreography to a particular version, and therefore rhythm, of Seeger's songs. "Many of the songs we knew, but not like this. Pete played them in different ways; he never played anything the same way twice," Ungar says with a laugh. A big part of what The Mammals had to do was to help Pete comport with his own originals.

When Merenda and Ungar held the first Hoot at Ashokan in the summer of 2013, Seeger arrived bright and early on a

The Mammals

sunny late-August weekend. Only a handful of people, many with small children, were there at 10 a.m. A lean, keen-eyed old man in khakis, a green shirt, and baseball cap (Seeger was always careful of the sun) went from group to group, greeting folks, chatting. He watched a juggler perform, and gave it a try himself. He stepped on stage to join Natalie Merchant, Elizabeth Mitchell, and Mitchell's daughter Storey Littleton for a song. In his own set, Seeger encouraged the children in particular to sing along. Standing on a stage named for his late wife — Toshi had died just over a month before — he led the audience in the verses she had written to "Turn! Turn! Turn!" for their children in the 1950s:

A time for dirt, a time for soap
A time for tears, a time for hope
A time for fall, a time for spring
A time to hear the robin sing.

After the show, Seeger returned home to Beacon and sent Ruth and Mike a postcard telling them that, next year, he'd be at The Hoot for more than just one day.

Carrying On

Pete died on Jan. 27, 2014, in New York City. He was 94. "There couldn't have been Pete Seeger alive and Trump's presidency in the same universe," says Merenda, in a voice both wry and rueful. Then he brightens, speaking of the renewed sense of purpose he learned — among many things — from the old master. "Pete was so sharp. He had this intuition to plant seeds. He didn't like being considered an icon, but he knew his words carried weight." This was true of what Seeger spoke in private and public, of the causes he espoused, and in the songs he chose to perform. "It's not only possible to speak your mind on stage, it's vital," Merenda says. "But watching the way he navigated an audience ... you pick your moment, get your point across. His message was laced

in every song he sang. He didn't need to hit you over the head." In a society too full of vitriol today, Merenda chooses Seeger's path: "Instead of harping on what we're against, it's more what we're for."

The sense of responsibility both for where he lived, and for those who listened to him and sought to follow, was in the end Pete Seeger's leading characteristic. Thanks to him, the Hudson Valley and the river running through it have returned to a place closer to the health and richness that drew human settlers here in the first place. And, thanks to him, people of every generation since his own, living in the area, sing out loud.

Renehan remembers a day with Seeger, not so long ago. "Once we were walking on that old downtown mall, the Main Mall, in Poughkeepsie. A kid, about 17, was playing a guitar with a hat in front of him. Pete said, 'I have to stop.' He had his banjo, and played a couple of songs with the kid. He told him, 'You're making some good music. Keep on.' " ■

OFF THE AIR

What Pete Seeger and Tom Morello's struggles say about censorship and fear

by Will Hodge

FOLK MUSIC HAS A WAY OF getting right to the heart of the matter, whether it's love, death, politics, or war. And for about as long as there have been airwaves to broadcast such pointed songs, there have been people who have sought to silence them. Whether it's Bob Dylan being told by CBS executives that he couldn't play "Talkin' John Birch Paranoid Blues" on *The Ed Sullivan Show*; Loretta Lynn's radio bans for songs like "Don't Come Home a Drinkin' (With Lovin' on Your Mind)," "Fist City," "The Pill," and others; or Dixie Chicks' career-throttling blacklisting after their comments opposing President George W. Bush in the lead-up to the 2003 invasion of Iraq, some of roots music's run-ins with censorship have happened on large-scale cultural platforms and in full view of the public eye. Perhaps no roots musician embodies this battle against the censors more than Pete Seeger, who defiantly fought for free speech in a variety of public spaces and even took the fight all the way to the US House of Representatives.

After a short stint singing topical, anti-war, and anti-racism folk songs in The Almanac Singers in the early 1940s,

Seeger co-founded The Weavers, one of the most influential folk groups of all time, in 1948 alongside fellow musicians Ronnie Gilbert, Lee Hays, and Fred Hellerman. The Weavers experienced increasing success with their revivalist recordings (with record sales in the millions) and rowdy sing-along concerts, even scoring a *Billboard* No. 1 for 13 weeks with their cover of Lead Belly's "Goodnight, Irene" in 1950.

While The Weavers were more concerned with folk song resurgence than political stances, the US was at the height of its second Red Scare and McCarthyism was in full swing. Within the fevered anti-communism climate, Seeger's critics — of which there were many — looked suspiciously on the pacifism and pro-labor thrust of his earlier career, and the fallout to Seeger and his new bandmates was swift and severe. The Weavers were officially blacklisted from television and radio, its members were all placed under FBI surveillance, their record label dropped them, and Seeger (along with Hellerman) was subpoenaed to appear before the House Un-American Activities Committee (HUAC), the congressional investigative body that conducted trials of

anyone suspected of having ties to communism or fascism.

Seeger testified before the HUAC on Aug. 18, 1955, and famously fought for his First Amendment rights by refusing to invoke his Fifth Amendment rights (a principled anomaly as "pleading the Fifth" was a common practice for many individuals brought before the HUAC). During the proceedings, Seeger refused to be bullied into "naming names" regarding his associations and affiliations, instead stating, "I love my country very dearly, and I greatly resent this implication that some of the places that I have sung and some of the people that I have known, and some of my opinions ... make me any less of an American." Because of this, Seeger was eventually indicted for contempt of Congress, found guilty by jury trial, and sentenced to a year in prison in 1961. Although Seeger never had to serve any jail time — his ruling was overturned on appeal in 1962 — he was still publicly and professionally blacklisted and unable to perform and record at the level he once did.

After his encounter with the HUAC, Seeger had another fairly high-profile battle with censorship, this time at the

Pete Seeger arrives at Federal Court in 1961 with his guitar over his shoulder.

Tom Morello during
Occupy Wall Street in 2011

hands of television executives. In 1967, Seeger was booked to play on *The Smothers Brothers Comedy Hour* — already notable for being the first television performance that would essentially end his blacklisting — and he chose to play a handful of numbers that included his new anti-war song, "Waist Deep in the Big Muddy," to protest the ongoing Vietnam War (sample lyric: "Every time I read the papers that old feeling comes on / We're waist deep in the Big Muddy and the big fool says to push on").

However, before the show was broadcast, CBS executives removed Seeger's performance of the individual song, leaving viewers to wonder why Seeger had played a banjo on the first song, conducted his interview holding an acoustic guitar, and then immediately played another song on the banjo. After a considerable amount of controversy played out in the newspapers (led by The Smothers Brothers themselves, who were strongly opposed to the censorship), CBS invited Seeger back to the show a few months later in 1968 to perform the song again for them to air in full.

Similar Experiences

"Pete Seeger was 'as advertised,'" says Tom Morello, fondly reminiscing on his interactions with the musical icon who passed away in early 2014. "He was friendly and welcoming in person but tireless and with a backbone of steel when it came to social justice issues. He was the glowing, positive heart and soul of folk music in America. I kind of came to folk music late, but I came to activism early. So his life and legacy as someone for whom music was a mission was very influential to me."

Morello may be best known for the otherworldly sonic alchemy he has created with his guitar in bands like the revolutionary rap-rock group Rage Against the Machine (RATM), Audioslave, and current supergroup Prophets of Rage, as well as in a few album appearances and touring dates with Bruce Springsteen and The E Street Band. He's also released three solo folk albums (and an EP mostly composed of covers) under the moniker The Nightwatchman, and most recently, an album under his own name — a multigenre, multiguest "Hendrix meets EDM" project titled *The Atlas Underground.*

Over the last few decades, Morello's instrumental talents, musical fearlessness, and charismatic charm have continually allowed him to create music in an impressive assortment of different sonic spaces and with an uncommonly diverse set of artists — including with Seeger himself. Morello shared the stage with Seeger on multiple occasions and even recorded a duet with him for Seeger's *A More Perfect Union* album in 2012.

In fact, Morello was so energized by Seeger's "one-man revolution" ethos that he named his first Nightwatchman album, which debuted in 2007, *One Man Revolution.* (The cover features Morello holding an acoustic guitar with the message "WHATEVER IT TAKES" on it, itself another ode to Seeger.) Morello's alignment with Seeger's activism and adaptability can be seen in how they both have pursued social justice on the ground in direct proximity to the need: "I was truly inspired by his embodiment of 'the one-man revolution,'" Morello says, "that with just an acoustic guitar, you can go to the front line of any struggle at any time, whether it's singing for voting rights in the Deep South in the 1960s or playing for bail money for anarchists in the 2010s."

Also like Seeger, Morello's career has also been marked by attempts at censorship and suppression. One of the more public examples of this took place in 1996, when Rage Against the Machine was set to play *Saturday Night Live* alongside (or, really, in diametric opposition to) the evening's host, billionaire businessman-turned-Republican-presidential-hopeful Steve Forbes. As the band was getting ready to play their first song, "Bulls on

> **"I was truly inspired by [Pete Seeger's] embodiment of 'the one-man revolution, that with just an acoustic guitar, you can go to the front line of any struggle at any time, whether it's singing for voting rights in the Deep South in the 1960s or playing for bail money for anarchists in the 2010s."**
>
> Tom Morello

Parade," some members of the RATM crew hung upside-down American flags on the band's amps — a common occurrence at RATM shows and a move that was meant to send a distress message reflecting the band's outlook on the state of America's (dis)union. After a brief pre-performance scuffle, the flags were removed and RATM played their song.

As Morello explains, after they got offstage, "There was a slight incident backstage, we were not allowed to play a second song, and we were summarily dumped on the sidewalk in front of NBC for all of our troubles." Though it's unclear whether Rage Against the Machine was officially banned from returning to *Saturday Night Live*, neither they nor any other of Morello's bands have been invited back to the *SNL* stage.

Beyond being blocked from displaying their upside-down flags, being denied their second song performance, and being physically escorted from the building, Morello sees a deeper ugliness to the whole debacle: "To me, that's where commerce and politics intersect. If you have ideas that run counter to the mainstream and that are 'bad for business,' then people are going to try and silence you. At the end of the day, do you really believe in what you believe in, and are you willing to pay that price for it?"

A few years later, in the aftermath of the 9/11 terrorist attacks, mass media conglomerate Clear Channel Communications sent a list out to the hundreds of radio stations they owned that featured songs that they deemed inappropriate and "strongly recommended" that the stations not play.

As Morello tells it: "It was a crazy list — songs like John Lennon's 'Imagine' to

The Gap Band's 'You Dropped A Bomb On Me' to The Bangles' 'Walk Like An Egyptian' were all banned. However, there was only one band whose entire catalog was stricken from every Clear Channel radio station, and that was us. It said 'all songs by Rage Against the Machine,' when, at the time, I would argue, those songs were most necessary to reflect on imperialism and what the US had been doing in the world that might cause someone to be so fed up to commit such a heinous act."

Looking back on Seeger's experiences with censorship, Morello views them as badges of honor: "If the House Un-American Activities Committee is pursuing you because of the songs you're singing, it probably means you're writing pretty good songs. When you make an example of someone like Pete Seeger — and he was heroic for standing up and not selling out in that instance — it's a warning to other artists who stand up against the powers that be. Pete Seeger was one person that they were trying to silence, but more broadly it was a warning that if you raise your head above the parapet, there's a real price to be paid."

Regarding Seeger's struggle with CBS over "Waist Deep in the Big Muddy," Morello finds a humorous irony not only in the network's failures to silence the folksinger, but also in the way their clumsy attempt at censorship actually drove more attention to the song that they were trying to keep off the air altogether.

"That was a clear example of 'give them enough rope and they'll hang themselves,'" says Morello with a laugh. "By making such a fuss about it, they definitely shined more light on it. The song is a chilling indictment of war and

particularly the immorality of America's involvement in the Vietnam War, and it's also a portrait of courage of someone who is steadfastly holding for their beliefs in light of a lot of pushback."

For Morello, the fact that a song would even be considered for censorship was proof enough of its ability to empower movements and strike fear in the hearts of leaders trying to maintain control: "It speaks to the fact that music can be dangerous and is viewed that way by the authorities. It does have a power beyond simple entertainment." He adds: "If you're making music that everyone can agree on and that no one has any inclination to try to block or censor, then you're probably making pretty shitty music."

Although there may be some auditory and aesthetic differences between Seeger's banjo-plucking and Morello's cranked-to-11 guitar pyrotechnics, the sometimes folkie, sometimes rap-rocker uses Seeger's own words to convey the comradery and kinship they have shared in the face of censorship: "It really is links in a chain. We're all different parts of the same cultural wing in the ongoing revolution for a more just and humane world. That battle is fought on many fronts, but on the cultural front, music has been a crucial component of every progressive and radical revolutionary success in this country. Pete was around for a lot of that.

"I remember seeing a picture of him in his 90s marching with Occupy Wall Street in New York. All the way to the end, he led a really inspiring life and was also just a very good dude. Pete Seeger is the golden conscience. He's the angel on every activist's shoulder." ∎

A GUIDING FORCE

The Kronos Quartet celebrates 100 years of Pete Seeger

by Hilary Saunders

LAST YEAR, VENERATED record label Smithsonian Folkways Recordings re-released Pete Seeger's *Goofing-Off Suite*. The 17-track collection, originally issued in 1955, features interpretations of works by Johann Sebastian Bach, Ludwig van Beethoven, Igor Stravinsky, and Edvard Grieg arranged for the five-string banjo, in addition to a number of traditional and folk tunes. The five classical works sit in the middle of Side A, slotted innocuously between the American marching song "The Girl I Left Behind Me" and a reprise of Seeger's introductory instrumental theme.

To listeners, it might seem strange to hear the lean and sometimes shaggy folk hero diving into the buttoned-up world of classical music. But according to Seeger, there's not really that much of a difference.

As he writes in the *Goofing-Off Suite* liner notes, "I am in favor of folk musicians swiping tunes from symphonies, just as I am all in favor of symphony composers continuing to swipe folk tunes. In time we may no longer think of different classes of music such as — folk music on one plane, popular music on another plane, and somewhere on another level, classical music. Rather, we are likely to have music for different purposes: lullabies, game songs, marches, music for dancing, love, work, storytelling, for participation, and for listening. Composers, arrangers, and performers, whether amateur or professional will have a vast heritage to draw upon, in the folk and fine arts music traditions of every continent."

David Harrington of The Kronos Quartet feels a kinship with Seeger in this way. For more than 40 years, the founder and first violinist of the experimental chamber quartet has been manipulating classical instruments outside of their traditional sounds and environments. The quartet has performed at rock shows, operas, avant-garde presentations, jazz festivals, and more. And this year, they've been commissioned to present multiple concerts in honor of Seeger's centennial — first at their own Kronos Festival in San Francisco in May and then at the FreshGrass Festival in North Adams, Massachusetts, in September.

Seated at a downstairs table in the Woolworth on 5th in downtown Nashville — a historic locale for lunch counter sit-in protests during the civil rights movement — Harrington never passes up a top-off on his coffee. He's been awake since four in the morning trying to learn more about Gandhi's favorite song, which later inspired Seeger. He lists just a few songs that Seeger either brought to the US or popularized domestically, including the Chilean "Estadio Chile," Cuban "Guantanamera," Israeli "Tzena, Tzena, Tzena," Irish "Kisses Sweeter Than Wine," and South African "Mbube (Wimoweh)." They're all folk songs in their own ways, but sonically, they're totally different.

"It's why you can't really define him,"

muses Harrington, "and I guess I feel really close to that."

The Creative Impulse

For The Kronos Quartet, the idea for honoring Seeger's centennial germinated about a year ago. Harrington had met Clarence Jones, who was Martin Luther King Jr.'s lawyer, researcher, and eventual speechwriter, and then worked with composer Zachary James Watkins to compose an original work featuring Jones. The piece, "Peace Be Till," was inspired by the moment Mahalia Jackson encouraged King to veer from his iconic "I Have a Dream" speech, which Jones helped write. The quartet performed the West Coast premiere of "Peace Be Till" at its own Kronos Festival in 2018, and after the performance, they closed with a version of "We Shall Overcome." When reprising "We Shall Overcome" during a San Francisco public elementary school concert just a few days later, Harrington realized that Seeger would have turned

100 this year.

By December 2018, Harrington was already seeking research materials, particularly multimedia from the American Folklife Center at the Library of Congress to incorporate into their Kronos Festival presentations. One Seeger-related element involved a public talk by Todd Harvey, a curator at the American Folklife Center. His 90-minute presentation, "Pete Seeger: 'The World that Music Lives In'" highlighted the troubadour's activism and involvement in social rights movements through a number of film archives.

"From our perspective at the Folklife Center, [this collaboration is] particularly relevant because it's part of the stewardship we take on with these materials — not just locking them away, but making sure they're accessible to artists and researchers and family members and the general public who is interested in this stuff. So I think it's important for us to be involved in this kind of activity for that very reason," says John Fenn, head of research and programs at the Folklife Center. "But also I think the creative use of stuff is always very exciting. It adds new life to it. And Pete and Toshi were certainly interested in the creative impulse and music and communities, so there's a nice parallel there that I see."

The Kronos Quartet also debuted at its May festival the first part of an original composition inspired by Seeger and commissioned by the FreshGrass Foundation (*No Depression*'s parent organization). The FreshGrass Composition Commission is a $50,000 award given each year, as the organization says, "to an artist whose work reflects the FreshGrass mission to preserve and support innovative grassroots music." The quartet played this new work written by the group's longtime composer, Jacob Garchik, as well as existing works that include elements of Seeger's songs and international pieces that Seeger helped bring into American popular music.

Harrington conceptualizes something even bigger for the rest of the project when it's performed at the FreshGrass Festival's Seeger-themed presentation titled "Kronos Quartet's Music for Change: Pete

Seeger @ 100." "We're trying to figure out a way to have a concert piece that includes a sing-along within the piece, which we've never done before," he says. After the FreshGrass Festival, he hopes that The Kronos Quartet can take this concert piece and perform it anywhere.

Additionally, FreshGrass Artists in Residence Aoife O'Donovan, Sam Amidon, and Lee Knight are expected to contribute to The Kronos Quartet's performance in September. Elements might even be recorded in the new studios at The Porches Inn, across the street from the museum.

But sitting in Woolworth, artfully mismatched in a black and white striped T-shirt under a green and blue plaid button-down with a No. 2 pencil sticking out of the pocket, eraser-side up, Harrington ponders how much there still is to do and how much will be left to spontaneity. "To really represent Seeger's work, we have to be open to what might happen, what might be come available even at the every last minute in terms of musicians," he says, wondering aloud if Mongolian folk group Hanggai, Malian desert blues band Tinariwen, or contemporary folk-rock stalwarts Iron & Wine and Calexico would be down to jam with them to Seeger's music.

But no one seems to worry about how these classical musicians will connect with diverse fans of these groups and more, especially via the work of a folksinger like Seeger.

"I hope that people take away this idea that genre lines are necessarily blurry and that's okay!" exudes Fenn. "And I think that people will also learn about the legacy of certainly Pete Seeger, but Toshi as well in their travels around the world and their embrace of musical diversity, and by extension, cultural democracy."

For Harrington, Seeger's boundless curiosity about people and culture informs his music, regardless of genre. "I'm thinking that this opportunity is not only going to expand the palate of Kronos, but hopefully it will expand instrumentally the palate of things that Pete Seeger himself did. I want to use his example as a guiding energy and a guiding force for what we do." ■

I'm With Her

JODY MARCH

ONE NIGHT IN 1968, THREE MEN sang at a party and changed folk music forever. The men were David Crosby, Stephen Stills, and Graham Nash, and over the course of their various collaborations, they'd realized their harmonies were impeccable. As to which party it was, it's less certain. Crosby and Nash swear it was Joni Mitchell's, but Stills believes it was Mama Cass', because he would have been way too nervous to sing for Joni Mitchell. Sometimes music history gets blurry. What's sure is that, with the addition of Neil Young, a legendary supergroup was born, leaving an indelible mark on a post-Beatles music scene that was hungry for new heroes, especially ones that brought social values of the 1960s into a new iteration of multipart harmony.

It's hard to overstate the mark Crosby, Stills, Nash, and Young (and all their permutations) have left. As The Milk Carton Kids' Joey Ryan told *The Boston Globe* in 2013, "There's nothing more exciting for me than listening to a Crosby, Stills & Nash album and trying to sing along with just one of them. It's impossible. ... You actually can't tell who's singing what, and because of that, the narrator of the song becomes not any of the real people who are singing, but rather the space between all of the people

FINDING HARMONY

The spontaneous, glorious lives of folk music supergroups

by Erin Lyndal Martin

contributing to this one voice you're hearing. So as a listener, you're engaging with somebody who's a bit of a ghost."

Supergroups exist in many genres, but folk music has proved especially fertile soil for such collaborations, in part because of looser notions of authorship. Historically, folk songs have passed through the oral tradition, including performances in song circles or around campfires. Since songs are shared more readily, the concept of authorship is less tied to an individual. The folk tradition is steeped in artists covering one another's songs. Being more open about the trajectory of a song lends itself beautifully to the sharing of ideas and the desire to find new manifestations of other artists' songs.

All for One

Supergroups foster not only a general sense of collaboration, but also teamwork among top-notch musicians. And oftentimes, working together helps improve an individual's skills. Cry Cry Cry, for example, began in 1998 as a trio project between Lucy Kaplansky, Richard Shindell, and Dar Williams. The three established musicians decided they would celebrate the thriving singer-songwriter environment of the '90s by playing the songs of their peers.

Jointly arranging and performing covers by R.E.M., Ron Sexsmith, Robert Earl Keen, and more helped sharpen the musicianship of the whole band. Says Williams, "It really tuned me up. Richard and Lucy really have amazing pitch. It tuned my ear. It helped me discover that I truly love singing harmony."

Williams also remembers going to folk festivals and song circles in pursuit of songs, which helped develop her listening skills as much as her musical ones. "It really fueled the next two

Voices on the Verge

decades of songwriting and inspiration for me," she says. "I was staring at trees and ducks and lonely people on park benches looking for my next song, but really the soaking in of all this great music from my peers from all over the country influenced me much more than I realized at the time."

Likewise, New York singer-songwriter Jess Klein believes that her time in Voices on the Verge — a musical collective of independent women that also included Beth Amsel, Erin McKeown, and Rose Polenzani — not only helped her develop her skills at collaboration and harmony, but also provided a new guitar role model. "I had to pay attention to what the others wanted from me as opposed to saying, 'This is my show.' Also, Erin [McKeown] was really good on electric guitar, and I remember thinking I didn't know what she was doing at all. It made me realize I needed to learn how to do that."

Such collaboration can come with its share of nerves, too, especially when the supergroup involves musical luminaries. Speaking about recording Bob Dylan's lost songs in supergroup The New Basement Tapes in 2014, My Morning Jacket frontman Jim James (who also released two solo albums last year) recalls anxiety about the impressive roster of collaborators. Producer T Bone Burnett had been gifted a box of Dylan's unrecorded lyrics, and he assembled a band including James, Elvis Costello, Rhiannon Giddens, Taylor Goldsmith, and Marcus Mumford to record at Capitol Studios. None of the members had met before, and they had the burden — but also the gift — of putting music to Dylan's lyrics.

For James, the nervousness about working with Costello dispelled as soon as the writing began. "I've seen a lot of people throw their ego around, but with him it was just so beautiful to work with him and see where he came from and how complex his songs could get," he says.

Remembering what it was like to share songs with Costello, he recalls that one person would say, "I got a song, it goes C-B-D" and we would try that for an hour or so. And then Elvis would be like, 'Okay, I got this song. It goes F# diminished ninth, C# diminished 17th,' all these crazy chords that I didn't understand. I'm writing all over this piece of paper with a marker as fast as I can trying to keep up with fucking Elvis Costello."

One for All

For some supergroups, maintaining individuality is paramount, where others downplay their individual reputations. The Traveling Wilburys famously used pseudonyms in the album credits to emphasize unity and the backstory they created for the Wilburys. (They even chose different names for the second album than the first. Tom Petty was Charlie T. Wilbury Jr. on the first album and Muddy Wilbury on the second, George Harrison was Nelson Wilbury and then Spike Wilbury, and Jeff Lynne was Otis Wilbury, then Clayton Wilbury.)

Sometimes merging identities is limited by the ability to merge sounds. In the Wilburys' lead single, "Handle with Care," Roy Orbison's unmistakable falsetto demands attention when it appears at 40 seconds in. Monsters of Folk — singer-songwriters M. Ward, James, and Conor Oberst and Mike Mogis of Bright Eyes — had similar experiences when working on their collaborative folk rock project between 2004 and 2010. They realized that their voices were so different that harmony wouldn't work and chose instead to trade off verses. "You listen and it's definitely Conor singing a song or it's definitely M singing a song or it's definitely me singing a song," James says. "It's not like we tried to start a polka band with all of us singing at the

same time."

More recently, when Sara Watkins, Sarah Jarosz, and Aoife O'Donovan merged to form I'm With Her in 2015, a democratic spirit informed every step. "We don't want to be a collection of individuals. We don't want to take turns being featured for the sake of taking turns. We don't want to be overly conscious of features and turn-taking. We want to have a band identity that's hopefully quite different from our individual records and careers," says Watkins.

For another supergroup, the Americana trio Redbird, Kris Delmhorst, Jeffrey Foucault, and Peter Mulvey chose a campfire-style approach. All three sing into the same microphone that they mounted on the ceiling of Foucault's home in Fort Atkinson, Wisconsin, so that it's pure coincidence whose voice listeners hear most strongly at any given moment. When Foucault and Mulvey sing together, their voices find a curious blend of harmony, as Foucault and Mulvey can sound identical one moment and then wholly different the next. "If you graphed out the waveform, you would probably see overlap in the middle of our range. The timbre of our voices is very similar in just one spot and then it gets pretty different as we get higher and lower," says Foucault.

Sharing Songs

Whether supergroups function as a monolith or a collection of individuals, they bring different approaches to songwriting and performing. Within these collaborations, part of the fun (for both members and audiences) is seeing if each member will bring their individual songs or if they'll co-write, if they'll play covers, or some combination of all three.

When Voices on the Verge teamed up in 1998, for example, the plan was that each member would perform their individual songs while others provided harmony. That project evolved out of the members sharing a manager and having played a single show together before recording *Live in Philadelphia* and going on tour. There hadn't been a lot of preparation leading up to it. "We never tried to come up with any new material," Jess Klein remembers. "We did the one album and I don't think there was every any talk of writing together."

Meanwhile, I'm With Her started by doing covers, a way for the members to practice arranging songs. Much of the distinction between group members lies in the fact that they play different instruments: Watkins plays fiddle, Jarosz plays mandolin and banjo, and O'Donovan plays guitar and piano. Later, co-writing was a natural way to extend their spirit of collaboration, blurring the lines of who contributed what so much that Watkins can't even remember.

"Something that makes performing these songs fun and celebratory is how quickly we've lost track of the ownership of those ideas," she says. "There are some things that I remember, like songs that came from my voice memos. But we were working

so quickly to write there wasn't a lot of conversation going into it. I enjoy these songs because I feel like they're very much shared."

In other supergroups, the artists worked out a balance of covers and original songs. On Redbird's record, Foucault, Mulvey, and Delmhorst each brought one individual song to sit alongside the covers. Redbird had hoped to channel the spirit of late-night hotel song circles from their previous tour. Cry Cry Cry also selected covers, but their aim was to celebrate the music of their peers. The record includes 11 covers and Shindell's song "The Ballad of Mary Magdalene," which Williams had already been performing live.

When Monsters of Folk assembled, their DIY aesthetic demanded co-writing. Their eponymous album consists of 15 co-written songs, but the group supplemented those songs live with work from their other projects — for purely logistical reasons. As James recalls, "We didn't have enough time to fill a show with our Monsters of Folk music, so we brought our own songs. In was fun not to be precious with it and just say 'I don't care if you guys don't completely nail this song.

Let's just have fun with it and do it in our own special way.'"

In that group, members took turn playing different instruments, including those they hadn't played before. They agreed that the four of them would create and record everything together with no outside musicians, and that constraint freed them to explore new sounds. That spirit of adventure is key for supergroups, especially for folk ones seeking to channel a live experience.

Short-term Shimmer

Though a lot of supergroups modestly decline the word "supergroup," there's often a mystique surrounding how successful musicians can put aside their own careers (and in some cases, egos) long enough to work together and make music that is wholly different than that what any member could make on their own. That question has been a constant for supergroups, whether it's CSN forming in 1968, Monsters of Folk teaming up in 2004, I'm With Her in 2015, or new amalgamations in 2019.

On their February debut, the collective known as Our Native

Monsters of Folk

Daughters released its debut album, fittingly called *Songs of Our Native Daughters*. Made up of Rhiannon Giddens, Amythyst Kiah, Leyla McCalla, and Allison Russell (Birds of Chicago), the songs bring forward stories from the past in original songs that contextualize the tensions of the present, crystallizing what it means to live through these times. But even amid such an ambitious project, most members have other projects happening concurrently: McCalla released her third solo album, *The Capitalist Blues* back in January and Giddens also released an LP with Francesco Turrisi, *there is no Other*, in May.

Russell also contributed to another folk supergroup this year, with her partner JT Nero of Birds of Chicago, as part of Luther Dickinson's Sisters of the Strawberry Moon project. For Dickinson (of The North Mississippi Allstars), the heart of the project included gathering

Birds of Chicago, Amy Helm, Amy LaVere, Shardé Thomas, and The Como Mamas together in his Mississippi studio, throwing them together and exploring new influences. They recorded in as few takes as possible and with minimal post-production, resulting in a 12-track album, *Solstice*.

By definition, a supergroup is a side project, and creating one relies on the alignment of schedules and record labels. Especially with the challenges of the modern music industry, the standard for folk supergroups is not how long they endure, but rather that they can come together at all. Since supergroups are composed of artists with their own recording and touring schedules, not to mention record label obligations, it's impossible to know how many albums a supergroup will release or how many shows they'll play, if they tour at all.

Again, the mythos surrounding a

group is often higher than their output. Both Our Native Daughters and Luther Dickinson and Sisters of the Strawberry Moon have performed a few concerts together, but for the most part their work has been communicated via recordings — left for listeners to consume and mythologize in their own ways.

Ask most casual listeners how many albums Crosby, Stills, Nash, and Young released as a foursome, and they'll almost certainly think it was more than three. Like Peter Doggett, author of the book *Crosby, Stills, Nash, and Young* says, "CSNY's commitment to their music and their audience will live longest. And the irony, of course, is that they were only able to maintain that commitment for a few months at a time. CSNY have only spent two of the last 50 years together, and the other 48 answering questions about when they're going to reunite." ∎

A NEW FOLK

An oral history of the so-called "freak folk" movement

by Beverly Bryan

"I don't like the term 'freak folk.' That bothers me because that to me was like a bastardization of the concept. I think there was a commercial-based motivator to an extent. There always is with these sort of things."

Matt Valentine

NE OF FOLK MUSIC'S MOST important functions is preservation. Before mass media, folk songs were the carriers of stories and culture, passed down orally from generation to generation. Nevertheless, it's important to remember that traditions and stories have always changed in the process of transmission, with each singer, or generation of singers, incorporating elements of their own and discarding others.

The contemporary folk scenes that flourished in the US and the UK during the 1960s and '70s had, by the '80s, become their own kind of establishment, and were swiftly aging out of relevance. Over the '80s and '90s, nearly every genre of mainstream music

from pop to rock seemed engaged in a loudness war. Soft-spoken singer-songwriters were all but drowned out. But as a new century dawned, a group of musicians emerged who refused to shout to be heard. They picked up acoustic guitars and banjos, sometimes only because they were handy, and began writing all kinds of odd, extremely intimate music that was informed by punk rock and post-modern art as much as it was by more traditional folk music. Young singers like Devendra Banhart, Joanna Newsom, and Iron & Wine started gathering listeners starved for gentleness, subtlety, and a little idiosyncrasy.

Unlike their predecessors, the new-school balladeers of the early 2000s

were not particularly concerned with preservation or folklore (or even politics, for that matter). The musicians themselves were only tangentially in dialogue with the folk that came before them, and the scene was iconoclastic, even freaky — leading to the genre label "freak folk." On the surface, this response seemed to dismantle tradition; however, on a more fundamental level, these artists were remaking folk music, in much the same way that punk transformed and revitalized rock. Perhaps without even intending to, they gave new life to some very old modes of expression.

One major touchstone of this movement was a compilation called *The Golden Apples of the Sun*, released by the now-defunct alternative culture magazine *Arthur* and curated by Devendra Banhart. In this oral history, *No Depression* talks to some of the people connected through the CD to find out where their strange songs came from and what happened next.

Next-Generation Outsiders

The folks who released influential albums in this style circa 2004 came of age in the '80s and '90s, listening to

absolutely everything. Many started out playing in rock bands. Some would hesitate to say they made folk music at all. When they did look back for inspiration, it was to more obscure and idiosyncratic artists of the previous generation, such as English cult-favorite singer-songwriter Vashti Bunyan and American folkie Michael Hurley. Sometimes they deliberately subverted expectations associated with folk music, but even when they did, they tapped into the deep roots of the folk tradition, creating enduring, heartfelt songs in the process.

JAY BABCOCK, EDITOR AND FOUNDER OF *ARTHUR* MAGAZINE: Matt Valentine is probably the core guy going all the way through this, because [his band] The Tower Recordings back in the '90s were doing all this stuff and coming forward and that never stops.

MATT VALENTINE: [The Tower Recordings] was a more avant-garde slant of folk, and by "folk," I say that loosely, more as just kind of like people-related music, you know? In the earlier part of the '90s, like '93, 1994, I was living in a loft space with P.G. Six [Pat Gubler] and Helen Rush and we just started hashing ideas around for our love of everything from

Pentangle across, like, ESP-Disk-type records. Our minds were really open to this ideology of having this folk music that wasn't so stiff, but we were also not coming at it from a protest angle. For us, the nature of doing the art was the politic.

KYLE FIELD, LITTLE WINGS: In the year 2000, 2001, I went on tour with The Microphones — Phil Elverum and Karl Blau. The tour with Phil and Karl was formative because we would kind of approach every night uniquely and the shows were in vastly different places. There was one show on the beach, for instance, in Santa Cruz around a bonfire, and maybe one hundred people came. Karl and Phil and I would all have our separate set, but each one of us would play with one another and there would be an on-the-spot game plan. I was like "OK, I'm going to start with this one song and then you guys grab my ankles and tip me over on my back and start dragging me through the sand, all the way to the ocean."

We were trying to write meaningful songs, but not just sit there with a guitar. We didn't want to be like people playing at a winery in a nice shirt that people are supposed to be entertained by, with just

Diane Cluck

Iron and Wine

an acoustic guitar and pretty singing. And so, there was, like, a samurai sword involved that cut a pumpkin in half, or, like, fake blood capsules, or a paper wall that we smashed through.

It was lo-fi too, because we had crummy guitars and it wasn't amplified and you probably couldn't even hear it that well. There probably were some really lousy aspects to it, but it felt exciting enough that we were taking that chance with the fidelity not quite being there. The spirit was the main thing.

SAM BEAM, IRON & WINE: I was into punk rock and whatever was going on at the time. I grew up in South Carolina. My parents' college party music was Motown, but it's hard to get away from country music, so it was kind of a big mix. I mean, I was definitely aware of things going on at the time, way into Cowboy Junkies and Palace Brothers, Songs: Ohia, all these people who are reinterpreting American songwriting.

There was definitely a deconstruction going on, if you hear Codeine and Low and all those people sort of totally deconstructing punk or post-rock, or whatever the fuck you want to call it, and getting down to elemental parts, where it didn't have to be fast and

loud to be heavy.

The things I was interested in expressing were expressed easily with the equipment that I had. I didn't need a lot of gear. It worked in my favor to get across what I wanted to, honestly.

ANDY CABIC, VETIVER: I lived with friends who were going to the [San Francisco] Art Institute at the time [he started Vetiver in the early 2000s] so I lived in a house with a lot of visual artists and that was a scene I kind of was hanging around. ... And then I was writing on my own and learning how to play acoustic guitar and I met Devendra and we hit it off, and it was through our friendship and his encouragement that I started playing as Vetiver. The first Vetiver shows were just the two of us.

I was also in a band at the time called Tussle where I played bass and it was an instrumental post-punk kind of band. That band was democratic, where all decisions were made by the four of us and all the songs were written together. So Vetiver was an outlet for me to just do my own thing and work with my interest in melody and songwriting. Writing songs in my bedroom and recording them on my four-track, that was how I was developing those songs. It wasn't out

of some purist interest in folk, although I was certainly discovering a lot of stuff, whether it be through reissues or just digging around at Amoeba [Records]. That's when Os Mutantes' stuff got reissued. That was a big deal. It was like hearing a new Beatles or something. The level of invention and creativity and playfulness and really catchy melodies and amazing fuzz sounds.

JAY BABCOCK: A lot of this stuff is really bizarrely quiet. Mainstream music at that time was like rap-rock and it's just really horrible. Everything was loud and obnoxious, and I always thought there was a sort of a refuge-taking element in going to these shows because they were so different. You go to a bar and people are sitting on the ground? I think that comes across in the recordings too.

'Golden Apples'

If there was a scene for this wave of folk, it was scattered and somewhat nomadic, connected mainly by shared sensibilities, shared tours and stages, and friendship. Banhart and Vetiver were based in San Francisco, Joanna Newsom was in Nevada City, California, and Cocorosie and Antony and the

Vetiver's Andy Cabic with Devendra Banhart circa 2004

Viking Moses

Johnsons were cutting their teeth in New York City's underground of music, poetry, and performance art.

Banhart, who had just started to gain attention for his minimal yet surreal tunes, sketched a rough map of this landscape when he curated *The Golden Apples of the Sun*. Released on CD through *Arthur* magazine's imprint Bastet in 2004, Banhart not only curated and assembled it, but also drew the album art and hand-lettered the liner notes. It connected the dots between the artists just mentioned and others, such as Little Wings, Diane Cluck, and Viking Moses, and the earlier generation of eccentric bards through a song of Banhart's featuring '60s singer-songwriter Vashti Bunyan, whom Banhart saw as a kindred spirit.

JAY BABCOCK: I paid attention to Devendra. We put him in the second issue of *Arthur*, which [was] in 2002. Because we did that and then stayed in touch for whatever reason, basically what was happening was, during 2003, Devendra kept sending me mail. He kept sending me CD-Rs of all this music that he thought I would be into. It could be emerging musicians and sometimes some old stuff that he'd found. I just

thought, "Why don't you make a compilation?"

Something about the way he was touring, the shows he was playing, the people that were showing up — basically other people found him and would give him their records and he would listen to it and go, "Wow, this is someone really interesting, and here's, oh, here's another one."

When he played, it was him half naked, ton of hair and an acoustic guitar, maybe a bottle of wine, and it wasn't a schtick. It was really very genuine. Devendra in that moment was extremely open and also approachable, and I think, because of that, a lot of people that may have been shy or naturally quiet or weird, they felt like he was a safe person to pass their work to, a kindred spirit.

ANDY CABIC: Devendra was always championing the work of his friends, and he still does this all the time. He champions the work he likes. [*The Golden Apples of the Sun*] came out through *Arthur*, right? So he knew that was a platform to show off the work of people that weren't getting attention. And it turned out to be re-pressed, you know, so it got out. I'm sure no one quite

knew that was going to happen. But it's just a collection of Devendra's friends and the music he liked at the time.

VASHTI BUNYAN: When I first heard from Devendra, I think he wrote to me via the record label and he sent a package of a tape of his songs and some of his drawings. When I heard the songs that he'd recorded on answering machines or whatever he could get his hands on, I just instantly loved them. What he was asking me was, because he was having a really hard time of it all, should he carry on with it. I got back to him saying "Of course, you must carry on with it."

We corresponded by email after that, and then he sent me this track asking me if I could add something to it. That was "Rejoicing in the Hands," and this was at the very beginning of my working with my own setup, recording in my own house, so I was able record my part over the top and send it back to him and his record manager. It was such a delight to do that. We hadn't met each other, but we could make a song together, or at least I could add a bit to his song, which was really exciting to me at that time. Then I met him when he came to sing in Glasgow about a year after that, and ever since we've been just very good friends.

I think the way that he understood [Bunyan's 1970 debut album *Just Another Diamond Day*] was what really gave me enough courage to carry on and do some more, because he really, really understood it. And, because he was the age that I was when I was making that music, it made it even more precious to me that he would understand it in the way that he did. It all sounds so trite, but it's the heart in it that I think that he understood and the genuineness of it, that it wasn't made up. I wasn't pretending to be something I wasn't.

[*The Golden Apples of the Sun*] allowed me to be in a musical world that I had always wanted to exist and hadn't when I was young. It was obviously people who, had they been around when I was their age, there would have been sympathy and empathy and who knows what different kind of music would have been made. I've read in a few interviews that Devendra was influenced by me, that Joanna Newsom was influenced by me, and that's not true. She hadn't even heard *Diamond Day* before she made *Milk-Eyed Mender*. What I have always maintained is that they gave me a place, not that I gave them anything, but they gave me a place to be, and *The Golden Apples of the Sun* gave me a place to be, and I was immensely grateful for that.

DIANE CLUCK: It was an interesting grouping because it drew in some people that I knew from New York, and then also this other world that Devendra was moving in, which is kind of more of a West Coast group of folks, who, a lot of them landed in New York. Six Organs of Admittance and Viking Moses and Josephine Foster, Espers, Jana [Hunter] and Entrance,

Jack Rose, Little Wings, Scout Niblett, Cocorosie, and [Anohni] are all people who I either played shows with or would go see them play in New York in smaller clubs. It's kind of like a loose zeitgeist-friendship group that was happening at the time.

BRENDON MASSEI, VIKING MOSES: I had maybe four or five friends on there, people who I had already known for a few years. Before anyone had coined the "freak folk" term, which kind of defined that movement or genre of music, I thought, "These are really diverse music styles." These are artists that aren't concentrated in a single community, but are spread out all over America and beyond. To me, it represents fragmented yet overlapping musical communities coming together and concentrating into something a lot bigger.

Defining Terms

While individual albums were often warmly received, when critics looked at the movement as a whole, even the most sympathetic articles could take on a vaguely bemused tone. Imperfect terms like "new weird America," "psych folk," "acid folk," and "freak folk" jostled in their reviews with broader constructions like "indie folk" as writers tried to corral what was happening. The unwieldy "new weird America" came from an article about the Brattleboro Free Folk Festival in Brattleboro, Vermont, written by David Keenan for *The Wire* in 2003. The term referred back to critic Greil Marcus' phrase "old, weird America," which he used to describe the quirkiness of early

Americana. Matt Valentine organized the festival and coined the term "free folk" to define the type of homemade experimental music that he and his cohort pursued, using "free" in the same sense as "free jazz." For whatever reason, "freak folk" was the term that stuck, whether or not anyone liked it.

JAY BABCOCK: Nobody likes that term ["freak folk"]. Nobody. I've never met a person who used it or liked it. If someone used that term in a conversation, that was like a sign of like, "Walk away from this person." If you look at any of of any of the articles that we ran or things we ever did, we never, ever use that term.

You could say folk, or psychedelic folk or weird folk.

If you look at the cover of the second issue of *Arthur*, we had an interview with Devendra and the cover says "Freaked Folknik Devendra Banhart is Here," or something like that. Sometimes I thought people took that and made it into a thing.

ANDY CABIC: A lot of people were not interested in being called "new weird America" or "freak folk" or whatever the terms were going around. I think you start to see the rise of internet journalism and the continuation of weak genre descriptions that don't really serve the music and that was happening right from the get-go with people using those terms.

LITTLE WINGS: The first time I might have heard [the term "freak folk"] was on that tour with Devendra. I was pleasantly ignorant to it up until that point and probably hadn't looked at a

Spin magazine in seven years or something. It felt like a scooping in from the top, in the grunge way. I was like, "Okay, so they've found their poster boy." They finally found someone who photographs well or whatever. When you do that, that's when you get the imitators coming in to be that, like, in order to be "freak folk." It's like "Me too. I'm freak folk too."

I honestly felt like [Devendra] was kind of poking fun at the idea at the same time, which I thought was cool. He's like, "Oh, *Spin* wants to interview me." I think he was making the parallel between "freak folk" and grunge. He was saying "So-and-so the new Alice in Chains and this person is Nirvana!" So, I think the whole time, almost in a Bob Dylan-ish way, he was kind of toying with it and not taking it super seriously.

MATT VALENTINE: The Brattleboro Free Folk Festival was a one-time-only thing and it was such a magical thing. The energy was so perfect at that time, it didn't seem like it could ever be topped. It just happened to be a successful thing on a really grassroots level. We were all really surprised and uplifted by it. I don't think it could happen again.

It took place over two days. There was Charalambides, Michael Hurley, Sunburned Hand of the Man, MV & EE, Jack Rose, Scorces, which was Heather Murray and Christina Carter, that was their duo, but they were joined by Paul Flaherty and Chris Corsano.

I don't like the term "freak folk." That bothers me because that to me was like a bastardization of the concept. I think there was a commercial-based

motivator to an extent. There always is with these sort of things. Nothing new, just, for me, because it was so close to the bone, I think it was an intriguing look at things. Also, I think there's a slight plagiarism too, because, there certainly wasn't any overlap with the free folk community.

VASHTI BUNYAN: What did I think when people started calling it "freak folk?" I think I probably was quite pleased that it wasn't just "folk." The culture when I was maybe late-20s, 30s ... people referred to each other, if they were slightly out there, as freaks, and it wasn't a derogatory term at all. It was just a collection of people who felt that they had sympathy with each other, and "Oh, yeah, he's a bit of a freak" didn't mean a bad thing. It meant "He's one of us." So when freak folk, the phrase, came along I thought "Well, that's kind of how you could describe it," but only if you knew that "freak" didn't mean something bad.

Growing Up

This wave of alternative folk that so desperately tried to avoid being pigeonholed as "freak folk" welcomed its audience to new possibilities of simple, melodic, lyrical music. Acts as diverse as Fleet Foxes and Woods sprang up in that cultural clearing, which still proliferates today.

Meanwhile, the gang from *Golden Apples of the Sun* continues making music, though in many cases, such as that of Joanna Newsom or Anohni (who formerly performed as Antony and The Johnsons), their music has evolved,

leading to new influences, bigger sounds, and bigger stages. As for others, Iron & Wine's Sam Beam recently performed the songs from his re-issued second album, *Our Endless Numbered Days*, with the National Symphony Orchestra (in stark contrast to his first murmurs into a four-track recorder). Viking Moses released his fifth album, *Cruel Child*, in April, and Little Wings has four albums he plans to release this year. Vetiver's Andy Cabic has been logging acoustic duo tours with Fruit Bats' Eric D. Johnson, and the two released an EP of live tracks in February. Devendra Banhart, for his part, has built a substantial discography since 2004 and also put together another compilation this year — a humble collection of demos recorded by friends that he thinks the world should hear.

Bunyan looks back fondly on the moment in time captured by *The Golden Apples of the Sun*. It gave her the impetus to record *Lookaftering*, the long-awaited follow-up to *Just Another Diamond Day*, with Banhart contributing guitar and Newsom playing some harp, among other collaborators. Still, she too has her eyes on the future, whatever it may bring.

"I'm very lucky and privileged to have been able to witness [this movement] because it was very special, this upsurge of a generous spirit," she says. "It was extraordinary to me and it gave me great hope for the future. I think that there's a little doubt in my mind now, but those people are still there and they still have that spirit about them. So who knows what will happen next. I really don't know." ■

Will Beeley

JESSE FISHER

A DREAM REDISCOVERED

Will Beeley returns to folk music after 40 years

by Duncan Cooper

Is it just the night callin' as it whistles through the pines?
Is the day to come a better one, is the final dream defined?
Is all this just a passing dream, left for someone else to find?
— Will Beeley, "Passing Dream" (1979)

N 1981, TWO YEARS AFTER WILL Beeley wrote "Passing Dream," he packed up his Guild D-15 acoustic guitar alongside 25 half-finished songs and locked the case for good, or so he thought. His wife, Vicki, was then pregnant with their second child. After nearly a decade, Beeley's publishing deal hadn't netted a single songwriting placement. He'd played a lot of gigs around Texas, but his two albums, *Gallivantin'* and *Passing Dream*, sold fewer than 1,000 copies in total. Beeley's career as a musician, he figured, was over.

By 2017, the Beeleys had firmly established themselves as a reliable team of truckers, alternating 11-hour shifts behind the wheel as they hauled liquid nitrogen and other cryogenics from sea to shining sea. He was 65, a grandpa, living on the verge of a heart attack, though he didn't know it yet. Occasionally, over the years, he'd get a call or letter to his adopted home in New Mexico all the way from places like Sweden or Japan, asking, "Are you *that* Will Beeley?"

Gallivantin', it turns out, had become a private press collectors' gem. Beeley was just a teenager when he recorded it in 1970, singing fingerpicked Bob Dylan a good half-decade after Dylan had gone

electric, two Buffy Sainte-Marie tunes, and very lonely originals like "And Then I'll Be Gone." To release the album, he had formed a label with his construction foreman, Bill Peña, to press up 200 copies and sell them out of the back of his car. Now, rare copies on the secondhand market were selling for nearly $1,000.

A few years ago, a digital copy made its way to Josh Rosenthal, founder of Tompkins Square Records, the Los Angeles-based hub for acoustic guitar music and folk reissues. Where once archivists like Alan Lomax and Harry Smith set out to preserve America's oral folk traditions, today independent archival labels like Tompkins, The Numero Group, and Dust-to-Digital give new life to important recordings that might otherwise be lost to history's great dollar bin — a crucial historical practice and continuation of the folk tradition in the age of infinite cheap streaming.

"Will doesn't have any artifice, that's the best thing about it," Rosenthal says. The label head initially mailed Beeley a letter and then the two connected by phone. Before long the offer to reissue Beeley's two albums digitally and on vinyl in 2017 turned into a plan to put the folk-singing trucker in a recording studio —

nearly 40 years since he'd last set foot in one — once again.

Peach Fuzz

Before Texas, Beeley's family lived in Southern Oregon, in a little town outside Medford called Golden Hill. Somebody found gold there in the 19th century, but the place never became much of a hub. "I was kind of a loner," Beeley recalls, speaking through his headset as he and Vicki hit the road after a drop-off. "I didn't really hang around that many people. That's one reason I picked up the acoustic guitar, instead of an instrument in a band, because I could take off and go."

By age 14 or 15, he was writing lyrics, and the guitar was a chance to put them to music. He'd take his instrument, walk deep into a field, and figure it out on his own. In high school, the family moved south, and Beeley caught then-local stars Townes Van Zandt and Bill Moss at a coffeehouse called Dougie's near San Antonio College. "I was amazed that they could make a living playing music," he says. "I wanted to do it, so that was what I did."

By the late 1960s, he was firmly a folkie. "I have always been fascinated by the singer-songwriters," Beeley says. "People like Tim Hardin, Bob Dylan, Gordon Lightfoot." After graduation, he found menial work in Houston, and in his spare time, with a patchy teenagers' beard, he recorded five or six albums — he can't quite remember — straight to disc in a studio in town. His aforementioned foreman was a fan, and he encouraged Beeley to pick the best tracks he'd done and re-record them for a proper release. "I feel in love with studio work," he says.

For a debut, *Gallivantin'* feels like it's caught between things. The weakest moments come when Beeley adopts a more baroque form of poetry — somewhat trendy in the early '70s — and the best are when there's gritty precision. Lines like "Clouds of filter humming in the menthol of the crime," from "Seasons Are of Never," can't quite decide which style they'd rather be.

Elsewhere, he sings about "being dead in just a year," and "life and death, a walking hell," but the bleakness is nowhere near as memorable as when he describes a beach trip with a crush on "Walk": "Barefoot on the seashore, the waves and foam came crashing / I look into your eyes to find that you are only napping." It's silly, and kind of surreal. What he sounds like, above all, is a fiercely talented kid.

"*Gallivantin'* was learning how to write songs," Beeley says. "There's a couple things looking back that I'm real proud of and a couple things where I'm like, Ee-yeww. But I was doing that when I wrote it. It's like anything, you want to make it better."

The album got picked up on independent radio stations and he played shows consistently. San Antonio was a military town, so many of the patrons there were G.I.s, and when they bought the record they took it with them overseas. More importantly, *Gallivantin'* found its way to the fledgling Malaco Records, based in Jackson, Mississippi, which signed Beeley as both a recording artist and songwriter. Within a year of self-releasing his first album, he was traveling to a state-of-the-art studio, singing his songs before a full band.

Face in the Crowd

There's a demo of a version of "Circle," from Beeley's 1979 Malaco album, *Passing Dream*, recorded in the early 2000s by the late Tommy Tate. Like Beeley, Tate was a songwriter in the small Malaco stable; he had a taste of solo success in 1972, when his "School of Love" cracked Billboard's R&B Top 30, but mostly he was behind the scenes, writing for artists like Isaac Hayes and, in the case of "Circle," recording reference vocals for the great Bobby "Blue" Bland, who passed away before he completed his take.

In the decades since *Passing Dream*, Malaco built itself into a well-regarded Southern soul label, and this is a proper soul version, with organs and crisp hits on the drum rim. Tate, a journeyman by any measure, is decisively patient in his delivery:

And when the circles all complete,
* and the dinners served on the plates*
They eat, maybe they'll remember all
* they've done*
They're growing older day by day
* and seeing their children growing*
* away*
As they sit in that home,
* no longer young*
Dying in their twilight years, one
partner dies, one partner peers
In loneliness to hear the sound to die
* alone.*

This cut is a prized possession of Wolf Stephenson, Malaco's co-founder and chief engineer. "'Circle' is one of my favorite songs ever," he says. "It's one of my biggest disappointments, all this time, that we weren't in a position to do more with it. Will was a caliber that would have demanded attention, had we had the financial clout or the business experience to get it for him."

Passing Dream is, compared to the sparseness of *Gallivantin'*, a cosmic leap. "By the time I wrote *Passing Dream*," Beeley says, "I was in the zone, as the kids would say." The album's precise, soul-inflected production presages the slick Nashville country sound of a decade later. The writing is confident, notably on the highlight "Rainy Sundays," a song about growing away from your partner that begins mid-sentence: "But I don't even know you." On the cover, Beeley's peach fuzz from *Gallivantin'* has grown into a prolific mustache; by Passing Dream, he'd had his first son, and his much deeper voice lends his romantic darkness serious gravity.

Somehow, though, the album landed with a thud. Beeley doesn't hold a grudge against Malaco for not being able to push it harder, or place the songs he wrote for them. "I've always felt extremely lucky, not only to be able to get the writing contract and the recording contract, but to be able to get in the studio a couple times to create something," he says. "Whether it came or didn't, that's always been immaterial. I got to go in and got to do it. I was standing in a line that not a lot of people got to stand in."

It was a case of the right stuff at the wrong time. "I'll be really honest with you," he adds. "There was just a ton of singer-songwriters back in those days. If you don't really stick out, you're just another face in the crowd. And unfortunately, I was just another face in the crowd." When he was hitting dead ends in music, failure brought depression, Beeley says. "But when I got away from it, it didn't bother me. It just wasn't that important. The thing that was important was my wife and my kids, and I just refocused everything to that."

After he locked away his guitar, Beeley found work adjacent to the music industry. For a while, he and Vicki ran a record shop, though it was a hard living when their prices could be so easily undercut by the chain store down the road. Most of their clientele was nightclubs, and after sufficiently impressing one manager, Beeley was offered a job as a DJ and talent booker. That's the work that took him to New Mexico, which he continued up until his 50th birthday, when his boss told him he was too old. So he started driving the truck.

Working Music

Running parallel with the railroad
  tracks down U.S. 85
El Paso on the left, Juarez on the right
I'm not sure this is the town that
  Marty sang about
It's more like 'Tom Thumb's Blues'
  with the rain wrung out.
Looking across the river, wondering
  what's on the other side
There's someone looking back at me
  with the same look in their eyes
A lot of things run parallel, you can
  only wonder why
Down on that highway, U.S. 85.
— *Will Beeley, "U.S. 85" (2017)*

Jerry David DeCicca

Records are time capsules of an artist's life. Every decision, every emotion, is the product of exactly who they were then. *Highways and Heart Attacks*, Beeley's album of new material out in June on Tompkins Square, is all that and more: It runs his personal history through a kaleidoscope. As a teenager, he sang about death, but hadn't ever really faced it. Some tunes on the album are brand new, others come directly from his old notebooks. Love songs that were pent up for 35 years are finally finding their place.

It's one thing to discover someone else's music, and the reissues already offered new listeners that chance. But on *Highways and Heart Attacks*, listeners have the incredible opportunity to hear Beeley rediscover himself.

Beeley recorded the album in San Antonio in April 2017, which gave him a chance to visit his mother, then in her 90s. The titular heart attack came shortly after he'd finished the album, when he was back on the road, after an expensive trailer of liquid helium he was supposed to pick up had somehow gone missing.

"The first person I called from the hospital was Jerry," he says with a laugh, referring to the album's 44-year-old producer, Jerry David DeCicca. "He had just done an album for Larry Jon Wilson, and he'd died. I said, 'You've gotta stop recording old guys.'"

Beeley does sound like an old guy on *Highways and Heart Attacks* — "somewhere between Clint Eastwood and Kermit the Frog," as he puts it. But it's more meaningful than that. The newly written songs came from Beeley as a grandfather, which makes for beautiful subject matter, as on "Singin' Lullabies," where he sings over tender violin: "I hope the Sandman's comin' cause I'm runnin' out of nursery rhymes." The older tracks take on an exciting new layer of meaning, like the line, "It's hard to understand the reasons when your dreams fall like ashes to the ground," from "Help Me Face the Days."

"I like people that sound timeless, like they fell out of the sky," said DeCicca, a producer and accomplished musician in his own right (namely with The Black Swans and as a solo artist, having released two fantastic albums — *Time the Teacher* and *Burning Daylight* — in 2018). "Will has the ability to understand who you are.

That's something most writers stumble with: They can come off as really journalistic or a little bit didactic. But his writing has this very humanitarian and very empathetic view of the world. There's no gibberish in Will Beeley songs."

Both Beeley and Tompkins Square's Rosenthal are hoping the new album will bring attention to Beeley's back catalog, so he can finally achieve his dream of having another artist record his songs. "That's the one thing on my bucket list," Beeley said. "I'm looking forward to the day I finally see my name in the writers credits on somebody's album." Norah Jones could easily take on *Passing Dream*'s smoky "Rainy Sundays," or Chris Stapleton the wistful "Jack Daniels" from *Highways and Heart Attacks*.

Music was Beeley's job until it wasn't, when life demanded steadier work. These days, his guitar is too big to take in the truck, especially with two people, but now that he's back in the groove he's been coming up with lyrics on the road to play through when he gets home. "I'm looking forward to the day that I can retire," he said, "so I can sit back and write songs." ∎

Telling our stories

by Raye Zaragoza

I fell in love with folk music in the backseat of a soon-to-be broken-down 1989 white Saab. With my forehead pressed against the left side window and my bare feet curled up on the seat, I would quietly sing along with a few select mixtape songs blasting from those car speakers as I looked out onto the elevated New Jersey highways.

My dad would sing, "Cat's in the cradle and the silver spoon little boy blue and the man in the moon" and "I've seen fire and I've seen rain" at the top of his lungs as the New York City skyline faded behind us. My dad is a California Mexican (with American Indian roots in Arizona) that ended up a New Yorker after a short stint in the city where he ended up meeting my New York-raised, Japanese/Taiwanese immigrant mother at a karate class. My dad always told us the story that my mom knocked him out in a roundhouse kick, and he had hearts flying around his head like those old cartoons. I've always hoped that this story was true.

My parents both grew up as outsiders: My mom's family was one of the only Asian-American families in Scarsdale,

New York, and my dad's was one of the only Mexican or Native families in Saratoga, California. My mom said she fell in love with my dad because they came from different worlds that met perfectly in the middle. They understood each other's struggles and complemented each other's strengths. "And he knew how to use chopsticks!" she would tell us happily. And then very seriously, she'd say,"Never marry a man who doesn't know how to use chopsticks!"

Instead of raising their three children in a suburban home, they decided to spend their limited funds on a 400-square-foot studio apartment in Greenwich Village. Whenever the city would suffocate my dad's California bones, we would load up the car and drive out to the Pennsylvania woods. I hated the confinement of the car rides, and would protest after 10 minutes, but I always fell silent once Harry Chapin or James Taylor came on. The way James Taylor sang about love — that's when I knew that I wanted to fall in love someday. The way Harry Chapin could write a song like a novel moved me unlike any of the music my third grade classmates would show me. When I

started writing songs as a teenager, I knew that above writing a catchy tune, I wanted to tell stories. I wanted to write three-and-a-half-minute novels like Harry Chapin. But I would tell my stories.

Growing up, I learned storytelling in many ways. Mariachi music took me on a journey of an entire tragic love story in six minutes. At the American Indian Community House in New York, I saw how a creation story could be told through dance or a drum. My mom and her mother told us cooking stories passed down through generations, and taught us how through food, we keep our stories and culture alive.

But some stories weren't so wonderful. My dad would tell us about how our American Indian Grandma Villa was taken from her people as a child, put into boarding school, and adopted out of the community. Grandma Villa didn't like to tell this story, and didn't share most of it until her last years. My father also told us many cautionary tales of uncles who lost their lives in racially motivated crimes. Sometimes I would insist on hearing stories that I knew my parents didn't want to tell. They endured a lot of hurt as minorities in America and they wanted to shield their children from the extent of it for as long as they could.

My favorite stories, however, were the ones about my aunts and and uncles who marched for the Latinx community and for peace during the Vietnam War. I always knew that my diverse upbringing, and the stories passed down to me, would shape my outlook on the world, and, eventually, affect my writing.

I got my start as a singer-songwriter pounding the same Bleecker Street pavement of my heroes and heroines. I would write songs all day, and either wait tables or play an open mic at night. It was magic. I really felt like I was living the New York struggling folksinger ideal of those that came before me. I dreamt of playing packed rooms at the Bitter End like Carole King and how cute boys in the audience would throw flowers at me and ask if my songs were about them.

But during the Standing Rock movement and the 2016 presidential election, I started writing social justice songs. I was 23, and for the first time, truly felt like an outsider in my own home country. The daughter of an immigrant and an Indigenous person in what they call "the great American melting pot," I finally understood the importance of the stories that had been passed down to me. The pot had finally boiled over.

I realized I have a duty as a young person of color to fight for the same things my mom, dad, aunts, uncles, grandparents, and great-grandparents were fighting for. As writers, they tell us to "write what we know." I finally started to dig deeper and write what I have always known.

Social justice songs are a vibrant tradition in folk music and deeply rooted in communities of color. My 2017 debut album *Fight For You* was a collection of stories about my life. I wrote about my parents' journey to find the American Dream, my Grandma Villa's story, traveling to Standing Rock to stand in solidarity against the Dakota Access Pipeline, and my journey to find my own voice as a woman of color in the United States. After releasing the album, many people applauded me for creating a concept album, a protest album. I was grateful for the recognition, but also confused by why anyone would view my work as a concept. All the songs were simply stories of my life and existence.

As I've continued to play music, I've realized that there are too few women of color in folk music. And those of us that are here are commonly labeled by our race in articles, interviews, and show listings. And live, we are often placed at the world music stage rather than the folk or Americana stage because we are people of color.

When *Fight For You* was released, I heard the word "niche" very frequently. It felt that I was being constantly reminded that my stories are only relatable to a small group of people, and could never been seen as appealing to a broader audience. It seems that since there are so few women of color in folk music — our stories and truths are yet to be seen as mainstream.

I've always been drawn to the folk music genre because it is the musical tradition of storytelling. I hope that though music, we can pave the way for all stories to be shared. Because we all have common truths — no matter where we, our parents, or our grandparents are from. We all have notes to sing, words to say, lessons to pass down, and stories to tell that deserve to be heard. ∎

FINDING BEAUTY

Miami duo Dracula use the past as a touchstone for the present

by Stefanie Fernández

ON TUESDAY NIGHT, ELI TAKES the bus to Dorys' house. Dorys has Mondays and Tuesdays off, so Eli braves the Miami rush hour traffic headed west from the Design District to rehearse. As Dracula, Eli Oviedo and Dorys Bello have been singing together under cover of night for 10 years now.

This Miami duo can be spotted playing at well-loved local institutions like Gramps or Churchill's (known affectionately by Oviedo as "Church"), but their favorite places to play are quieter: beds, bathrooms, gardens, cemeteries, funeral homes. "It's like meditating under a waterfall," Oviedo says of playing at the louder venues. But regardless of the setting, you'll almost always find the two looking directly at each other as they sing upon their chosen stage.

In 2005, Oviedo was a server at an Indonesian restaurant downtown. He was studying at Miami Dade College after dropping out of the University of Miami, where he had studied music. He started his first band with a dishwasher at the restaurant, through whom he met Bello. Oviedo and Bello attended the same shows at the quirky, DIY spaces of Miami past like The Firefly. Meeting right as the two were coming into their musical abilities is a coming-of-age moment in Oviedo's memory.

That year also marked the opening of Sweat Records, the city's beloved record store and home for all things Miami music. In 2018, its founder, Lauren Reskin, launched Sweat Records Records, a homegrown independent label catering to pressing vinyl for Miami's best-loved artists. Reskin encouraged Bello and Oviedo to put their ephemeral, almost exclusively live repertoire to wax, enlisting the help of Andrew Yeomanson (DJ Le Spam and founder of The Spam All-Stars) to produce it, his City of Progress Studios to record it, and SunPress Vinyl to press it. The result was Dracula's official debut recording, *Dorys & Eli* — a collection of 13 acoustic covers in three languages (English, Spanish, and Japanese) that recontextualizes place, tradition, and genre.

Chasing Heritage

Born in San Pedro Sula, Honduras, Oviedo was raised in a fundamentalist Pentecostal household by a father who plays the guitar at church and a mother who sings. He wasn't really allowed to listen to secular music growing up, but sang in choir at church.

Bello grew up singing in the Miami Children's Choir, but stage fright eventually gripped her. She made bedroom recordings on MySpace as Softmonster (what she calls "pre-SoundCloud stuff"), and though friends asked her to play live, she flatly refused for years. "I would have died," she says.

Bello doesn't know what made her

play for the first time in public with Oviedo in the house behind The Firefly in 2009, except for wine. To alleviate the nerves, she began to obscure herself entirely beneath a lace sheet. People thought it was part of a somber, goth aesthetic. After a while, she would fold the sheet over her head so her face was visible, looking "like a Virgin Mary," she says, which people also thought was intentional. Eventually, she abandoned the sheet completely.

The first song Bello and Oviedo ever played together in 2009 was "500 Miles," the first of many Peter, Paul and Mary covers. They bonded instantly over a love of Vashti Bunyan and Françoise Hardy, but it was their parents' old records (and all the mom-love of Julio Iglesias) that made Dracula feel like family. "You'd go to a Christmas party, you'd go to a birthday party, and the parents would play all those Latin hits like 'El Perrito,' and 'El Venao,'" Bello says with a laugh, as Oviedo chimes in with "El General" and "El Tiburón." The formula has remained the same over a decade, their two voices and Oviedo's nylon string guitar. Oviedo's playing technique is fine, precise, and highlights his training in the Spanish classical tradition.

It took them both a long time to come to terms with exactly who they were, especially in Miami, where the city's majority-minority population can alter perceptions of the greater United States. "We really are our own country," Bello says of Miami.

Oviedo remembers hearing his father play *rancheras* and *corridas* and dismissing them as *naco* — uncool or unrefined. Bello's first language was Spanish, and she grew up with Cuban parents in Hialeah, where she learned English from watching Nickelodeon. She remembers a field trip to Disney World, where she saw a class of white kids getting off a bus and exclaimed to a friend, "Look, American kids!"

That feeling of otherness, even when surrounded by people like them, informed the songs Dracula built into its repertoire, the core that made it to *Dorys & Eli*. They're songs heard in living rooms among people who've shared a loss or an exodus, those stories palpable in the sparseness of the instrumentation in tracks that hover around two or three minutes in length.

Spiritual Lineage

In the early days, Dracula tried singing one of Oviedo's father's church hymns, a psalm. "It still felt safe to be singing songs that had that spiritual lineage," he says, even if he didn't really believe in them anymore. "Te Exaltaré / Las Diez Vírgenes" on *Dorys & Eli* comprises two hymns his father plays at church in a medley, as is his habit. For Oviedo, singing this music is "remembering what music sounded like to me when I first moved to the United States."

This spirituality and near-holy reverence for one's ancestry runs deep through *Dorys & Eli*, which came out in April. The album opens with "La Zenaida," a Mexican *norteño* song beloved by mariachis and Oviedo's father, who plays guitar on this track and "Rose Hip November," the running arpeggio lilting over a trumpet interlude. As Oviedo grew older, the music of Mexico, the more prominent of the Mesoamerican cultures, became a vector for better understanding his own culture and taking pride in it. "[It made] my family, and especially my father, make a lot more sense to me, and I guess myself, too."

Selena's "Como La Flor" had the same effect. As a kid, Oviedo just wanted to dance to it, but it was a "girl's song," overt in its imagery and emotion. Bello and Oviedo, however, slow Selena's Tejano cumbia-pop original to a ballad, stripping the pop and dance elements to isolate the mournful lyrics. "Yo sé perder" ("I know how to lose" or "I know loss") is less the confident affirmation of the original than an elegiac anticipation of another loss.

The same spirit drew them to secular American songs by Peter, Paul and Mary and Bob Dylan, as well as Pete Seeger's "If I Had a Hammer (The Hammer Song)" — all agents of healing in times of global suffering.

After listening to *Dorys & Eli*, Alexandro Hernández, an ethnomusicologist and lecturer in Chicano music at University of California, Los Angeles (and member of post-punk band ¡Aparato!) heard an implicit parallel between Dracula's music and *nueva canción*. This Spanish and Latin American movement of the 1960s committed itself to protest and social justice, with musical contemporaries aligning with Peter, Paul and Mary and Vashti Bunyan. In Chile and Argentina, for instance, *milonga, cueca*, and *marinera* music scored songs protesting Vietnam. In the Caribbean, it was known as *nueva trova* and popularized by musicians like Pablo Milanés and Silvio Rodríguez. In tandem with *nueva canción*, it built on the Cuban *trova tradition* of the late 19th and early 20th century, pioneered by songwriters like Maria Teresa Vera. She wrote "Veinte Años," a song Dracula sees as about the decline of not only romantic, but also familial love over 20 years.

However, says Hernández, "the harmonies [Bello and Oviedo] use aren't as standard in Latin American folk music." The English songs influence the inflection and precise harmony they use in, say, "La Llorona," though harmonies themselves are common in *rancheras*.

And vice versa: "Descripción," a gem by early '70s Colombian cult favorite Elia y Elizabeth, is a ballad originally influenced by psychedelic rock, but Dracula backs it with a rolling dance rhythm akin to Andean *huayno*.

The English-language songs on the album have roots in the Appalachian, Irish, or English folk traditions, but are coded with experiences of Latinidad (Latin identity) or being gay. Bello and Oviedo describe their rendition of the English traditional song "Butcher Boy" as a song for people who've experienced any kind of exodus (and change the "cherries on an apple tree" paradox in the lyrics to "mangoes on a banyan tree"). Their take on Peter, Paul and Mary's "Tiny Sparrow" is a warning song to women about flighty men, but Oviedo interprets it too as a warning of the personal and social perils of men loving men. They chose to sing the murder ballad "Down in the Willow Garden" (after The Everly Brothers version) to foreground historic and present-day violence against women.

"Typically, we see interpretations by a predominantly English-speaking artist of Latin music," Hernández says. "We don't often hear interpretations of Latinos doing country music or Americana." And the cross-pollination of these Latin American genres is neither an accident nor without precedent. Hernández cites Lydia Mendoza, one of the earliest recorded Tejano artists, and her 1934 recording of "Mal Hombre." That song is an Argentine tango, but with no access to an ensemble, Mendoza transmuted the form into a Tejano adaptation on the guitar.

Similarly, by quelling the volume and instrumentation traditionally associated with mariachi and *rancheras*, Dracula fills the space with the shape of trauma and loss that is passed down generationally in immigrant families. A distinctly Latin attitude toward death and its nearness persists on *Dorys & Eli*, but it's not sad. By covering songs made famous by Bunyan and Peter, Paul and Mary, they represent the themes of loss of country or identity that are intrinsic to English, Irish, Appalachian, and other folk for a new century.

But for Bello, it's especially important to her that her parents could understand and recognize Dracula's songs. Oviedo adds, "all the nameless, random people that my dad ever played with when we first moved to this country" are as vital an influence as all their favorite folk artists that differentiated the two from their peers. For folk, a genre now so intimately associated with native soil, Dracula conjures its roots from displacement.

"We found them beautiful," Bello says of the songs, and the exiles behind them. ∎

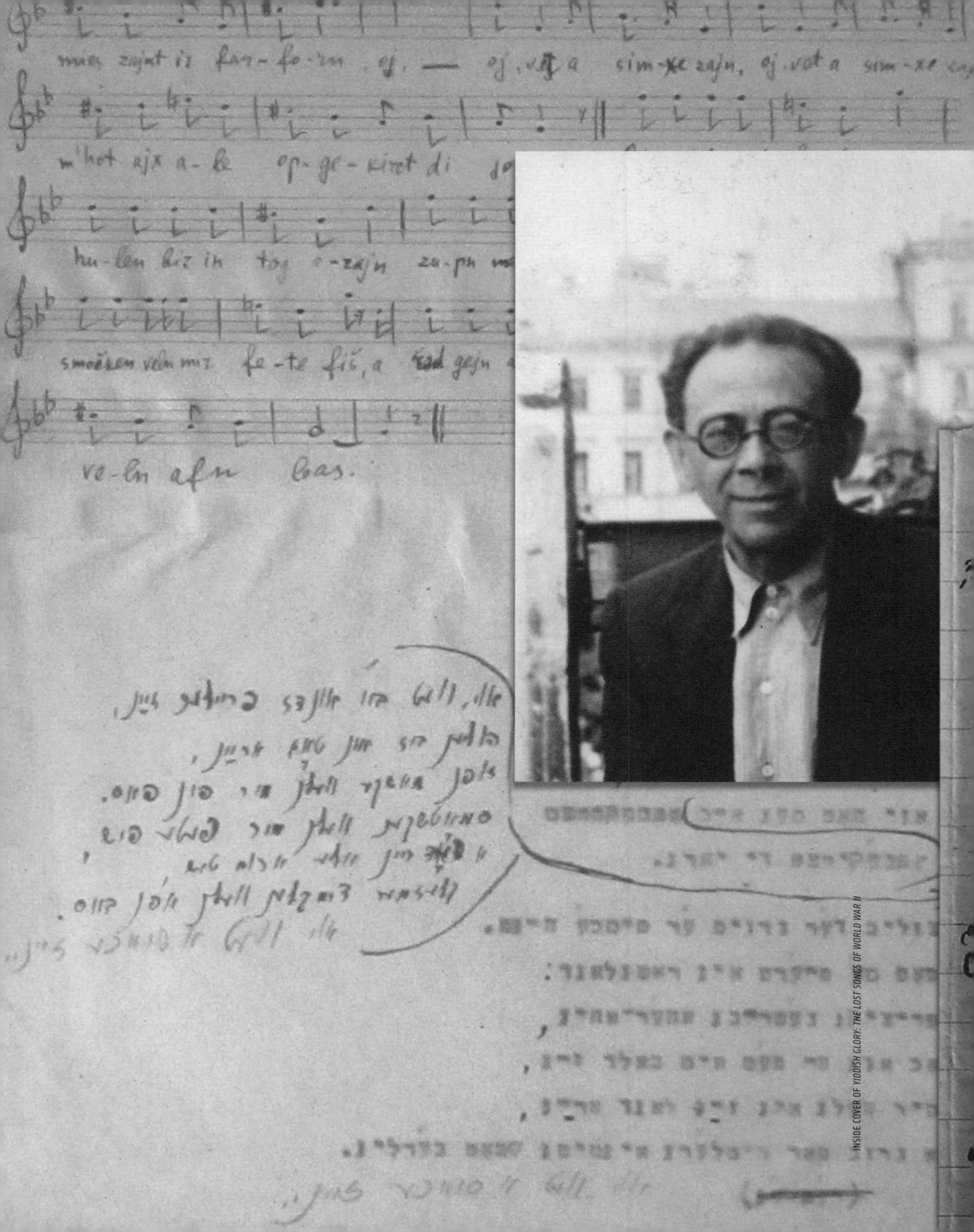

INSIDE COVER OF *YIDDISH GLORY: THE LOST SONGS OF WORLD WAR II*

SECRET VOICES

**Yiddish folk music and the stories
that connect generations**

by Hilary Saunders

"I'm not interested in fighting these battles because they're old. I'm interested in fighting them because they didn't get old. They're the same battles that we're fighting today. These old stories, these old songs have something to say to us today and we can let them inform our new songs."

Daniel Khan

Many Jewish children have grandparents who came from the old country. The Yiddish songs on this record were sung by such grandmothers and grandfathers when they were children in Eastern Europe. When we sing them now, it is as it we were paying a visit to the little town or village where they were born, in the old country.

THIS EXCERPT COMES FROM the liner notes of a 1957 album called *Jewish Children's Songs and Games*, released on Folkways Records, and later acquired by Smithsonian Folkways. The album features mostly secular songs remembered and sung by renowned author, singer, and folk song collector Ruth Rubin, accompanied by the legendary Pete Seeger on banjo.

Seeger's five-string banjo work presents a seemingly incongruous musical accompaniment to these songs — usually less-than-two-minute, minor key ditties about riddles ("Du Maydeleh Du Fines"), snacks ("Homntashn"), or games ('Shpits-Boydim') like the poor, Eastern European equivalent of "Farmer in the Dell." Rubin's warbling soprano, however, highlights a language that, in 2019, only about 700,000 people in the world still speak.

Yiddish, which is thought to have originated in the 10th century, is a language that was spoken by Ashkenazic Jews (those from Central and Eastern Europe). While written in the Aramaic alphabet, much of the language itself pilfered words from other Slavic, Germanic, and Romance languages as Jews fled from Western European countries toward Germany. It's a linguistic mutt, a secret tongue of strong consonants and phlegmy throat sounds that almost every Jewish person could speak, regardless of their country of origin.

In the early 20th century, Yiddish thrived through literature, poetry, and theater performances, especially in Russia. However, the Soviet government began to censor the language in the late 1930s, foreshadowing the Holocaust, which murdered six million Jews and decimated the spread of the language. Survivors, especially those who came to the United States, hastened to learn English and minimize their use of

Yiddish in order to assimilate and avoid any racist or lowbrow assumptions.

After the Holocaust, Rubin made it a personal mission to preserve as much Yiddish language and culture as possible, especially through Yiddish folk songs. One of the first women to become a prominent folklorist, Rubin collected more than 2,000 songs in her lifetime, often *schlepping* a hulking reel-to-reel recording device to the homes of Jewish-American immigrants from various "old countries" to capture their melodies and memories. She recorded three albums now available on Smithsonian Folkways, including the introductory 18-track *Yiddish Folk Songs*, which celebrated its 40th anniversary last year.

After Rubin passed away in 2000, Seeger was quoted in her obituary from *The New York Times* as saying, "She didn't try and put on any great airs. ... She just sang a song very simply. She was mainly interested in seeing that the song got out so that other people would learn it and sing."

Like Seeger prophesized, Rubin's influence remains invaluable in this small musical community, as her collected, transcribed, translated, and recorded works have helped newer generations reclaim these folk songs and spur another wave of interest in the language and music.

Don't Call It a Comeback

Actor and musician Jamie Elman is quick to caution, "People will not like the term 'Yiddish revival.'"

Elman, along with fellow actor and composer Eli Batalion, co-created and stars in the web series *YidLife Crisis*, a hilarious take on the existential crises many young Jews face between honoring tradition and 21st-century assimilation, which is delivered completely in Yiddish with English (and French) subtitles. The series began in 2014 and has featured episodes with Mayim Bialik (*Big Bang Theory*) and comedian and television host Howie Mandel. The duo also takes their *schtick* on the road as *YidLife Live!*, pairing their videos with stand-up routines and live musical performances.

Yiddish language experienced a small comeback in the 1970s, mainly through film and theater. And today, the vernacular is more accessible through popular television shows like *Transparent, The Marvelous Mrs. Maisel*, and even *Broad City*. A number of words have even entered English vernacular, like the *lox* and *schmear* (smoked salmon and cream cheese) on your bagel or the *schmoozing* (socializing) you do at parties.

Musically, however, a groundswell seems to be rumbling yet again. Over the past few years, an international community of musicians has released all kinds of Yiddish-language records that borrow from the old texts while embracing contemporary arrangements and styles. And while Yiddish punk and metal have emerged recently, folk music remains the most common musical style.

As a genre, ethnic folk music is already relegated to the outskirts of pop culture. And Yiddish folk music is an especially niche segment of an already niche language and culture. It's not surprising, then, that many prominent players already know each other, have gigged with each other, and support each other's work.

Although they grew up Jewish in Montreal and studied Yiddish in high school, Elman and Batalion never pursued this part of their culture in their professional work until *YidLife Crisis*. "Until we were aware of the entire world of Yiddishkayt [Yiddish folk culture] and Yiddish language music and theater

Songs from *Yiddish Glory* performed live. From left, Psoy Korolenko, Sophie Milman, and Isaac Rosenberg

and art and everything that's going on ... neither of us really knew anything going into it," says Elman.

"One big thing that we were aware of is the musician and renaissance man, contemporary of ours, Josh Dolgin, aka Socalled," he continues. Socalled took a classic Yiddish tune, "Mayn Shtetele, Belz" and sampled it in his own remake called "(Rock the) Belz." "We used it as a temp track as we were cutting episode one and then we realized this is the perfect song for us to actually use as the theme song for our show because it's doing [the same] thing: It's using Old World Yiddish and combining it in a new, modern way and we felt very aligned with him," says Elman.

"Mayn Shtetele, Belz," which translates to "My Little Town of Belz," is a nostalgic ode to one's hometown. In this case, the *shtetl* (small, poor, primarily Jewish town in Eastern Europe before World War II) is a real town in Western Ukraine near the Polish border. And the most famous version of the song itself, recorded by actor, producer, and folksinger Theodore Bikel (who also happened to co-found the Newport Folk Festival with Pete Seeger), sounds like the "Wedding Dance" from *Fiddler on the Roof* with its gradually accelerating

pace and chants of "oy, oy, oy, oy."

Socalled's "(Rock the) Belz," released in 2005, is a completely new take on the song. He keeps the "oy's" and the lyrics from the original chorus but recalibrates it for modern ears. An arpeggiated piano line underpins the entire song, playing softly solo before the drum kit percussion starts and the subtle record scratches hit. Socalled parlays American English hip-hop vernacular between the Yiddish samples, even delivering an entire original verse in English and closing out the track with calls to "Rock the Belz!" and "Holla at ya boy!"

Dolgin, based in Montreal (like Batalion and the setting for *YidLife Crisis*), has been making music under the Socalled moniker since 2003. While studying literature and philosophy at McGill University, he began making beats and searching for old records to sample. In a Salvation Army store near campus and in garbage cans around the city, Dolgin accidentally stumbled into a world of Yiddish theater music, klezmer music, cantorial music, and Hasidic music, all on discarded vinyl.

"I wanted to represent my self in hip-hop and I was making beats and I was sampling from where hip-hop is

normally sampled from, which is normally African American music — funk and soul and disco, basically inner-city African American music — and I was this Jewish kid in Canada in basically the country," Dolgin says. Around that time, he and his friends were listening to a lot of golden age hip-hop, and he cites The Wu-Tang Clan, The Notorious B. I. G., and Tupac Shakur as major influences.

"It was cool, but I also felt like hip-hop is about representing where you're from and who you are and your past and your musical ancestors and your own culture," continues Dolgin. "I would sample from my parents' record collection and took stuff from what they had, which did include some folk music and some Russian folk music and Eastern European music and that Theodore Bikel record (that one Yiddish record that we had), and it was a way to keep it real with the hip-hop I was making. But also, I was just looking for cool sounds that weren't being used by everybody else and looking for cool riffs and loops that were catchy."

In addition to his hip-hop oeuvre, Dolgin is also an accomplished pianist and accordion player, filmmaker and producer, and puppeteer. His most

Tsibele

recent album, 2018's *Di Frosh* (*The Frog*), features 13 traditional Yiddish folk songs performed in a modern classical style with the German Kaiser Quartett. Dolgin soothes the harsh edges from the Yiddish language while singing on *Di Frosh*. His even timbre and careful melodies help focus attention to how his voice intertwines with the chamber ensemble — another way Socalled continues the Yiddish folk tradition of merging the old and the new.

Generations of Song

Like Socalled, Daniel Kahn has been mining the troves of Yiddish language music since the early 2000s. With his band, The Painted Bird, Kahn performs a mix of radical klezmer-tinged folk-punk. His latest album, 2017's *The Butcher's Share*, is evocative of Billy Bragg with a woodwind section or early Frank Turner with a bombastic marching band bass drum. Some tracks are in English, some are new translations of old Yiddish, and some include lyrics in both languages.

Although born in Detroit, Kahn now lives in Berlin. However, when we speak, he's walking along Orchard Street in New York's Lower East Side, having performed at Carnegie Hall the night prior during a concert called "From Shtetl to Stage: A Celebration of Yiddish Music and Culture."

Kahn points out that many other musicians have preceded him in seeking Yiddish folk song traditions. In fact, that multigenerational tie of both the American folk tradition and his own cultural tradition steered him to Yiddish music while in his 20s.

"One of the beautiful things about the Yiddish music scene — and I think that this is something that it shares with other folk revivals — has to do with two tendencies. One of them is a tradition of subversion and [the other is] a celebration of subversive traditions," he says. "So that means you have new generations of creative folks who are constantly breaking with one part of the past and also carrying on other parts of the past. And rather than this building walls between generations, I find that it actually builds important bridges between generations."

Most musicians interested in Yiddish folk songs don't have the language skills to write their own lyrics, so they look to the archives of those who documented it before them (like Ruth Rubin, Ethel Raim, and a small cadre of scholars studying Yiddish culture from other academic perspectives) to find the words and their translations. Although Elman and Batalion studied Yiddish in school, neither Dolgin nor Kahn grew up with anything more than a few secret words from their parents or grandparents. The Brooklyn-based quintet Tsibele (which is the Yiddish word for "onion") is another group that has created new arrangements to old Yiddish songs. Violinist and co-founder Zoë Aqua knew a few words and tunes from growing up in a family that performed in a klezmer band, but has only recently started to take Yiddish language classes at The Workman's Circle in New York City.

In order for most of these musicians to move forward, they have to look to the songs of the past. As Kahn says, "Josh [Socalled] brings hip-hop to bear in this new culture and Tsibele, they bring a punk-folk-feminism to what they do. And we all try to do it with humor and respect, but also without being fucking precious or sentimental. And the last thing we are is nostalgic. Learning about this history is that history is not really a place you want to visit and you certainly wouldn't want to live there!"

Daniel Kahn

Socalled

Songs of Dissent

One reason why Yiddish folk songs are so difficult to categorize is because the language itself represents a diasporic people of a shared religion and culture, but of disparate socio-political contexts. There are folk texts and folk songs, and both come from many musical, geographic, secular, and liturgical sources. It's also why newer performers of Yiddish folk music struggle with differentiating types of songs and their own modern versions of them.

When asked to describe what Yiddish music means to them, Batalion of *YidLife Crisis* responds, "That's a juicy one, a *zaftik* one as you say in Yiddish!"

Batalion mentions four types of traditions that he sees contributing to the canon of Yiddish folk songs — klezmer music, religious music and songs about Jewish life, Yiddish theater, and a category that he says "can be too grossly described as leftist ideological music" and includes "culturally Jewish [music], mixed with Eastern European roots that have nothing to do with Judaism, mixed with leftist radicalism, Bundism, communism, [and] various revolutionary and resistance-based

traditions of songs."

This radical Yiddish folk music is likely the most popular version that has gained traction in the past few years, due to a rise in nationalist movements, anti-immigrant sentiment, and violent racist, sexist, homophobic, and anti-Semitic and anti-Islamic acts. Sometimes the radicalism appears musically, like in Socalled's genre-non-conformist work, but more often, the lyrics highlight leftist and liberal social beliefs, as exemplified on Daniel Kahn & The Painted Bird and Tsibele's albums. Tsibele for example, describes its 2017 debut , *It's Dark Outside – Indroysn iz Finster*, on its Bandcamp page as "Yiddish songs on life under capitalism, tyranny and hetero-patriarchy."

Says Kahn, "The first songs that I fell in love with were the songs of the immigrants who populated these streets and who worked in these sweatshops and who fought for workers' rights and women's rights, and who also fought for the dignity of their own language and culture in the face of assimilation. So that's all really inspiring in terms of the past, but I wouldn't have been so into this scene if the community of creative of people

who are working with this material aren't so radical and so personal in their approach. I'm not interested in fighting these battles because they're old. I'm interested in fighting them because they didn't get old. They're the same battles that we're fighting today. These old stories, these old songs have something to say to us today and we can let them inform our new songs."

Another recent example comes from last year's compilation titled *Yiddish Glory: The Lost Songs of World War II*. The album featured part of a presumed-lost collection of Yiddish tunes that Soviet Yiddish scholars collected during the 1940s in order to preserve the culture at the height of modern persecution. After 21st century academics found the archives, they resurrected these firsthand accounts of the ravages of war ("Mayn Pulemyot" or "My Machine Gun"), protests of occupation ("Misha Tserayst Hitlers Daytchland" or "Misha Tears Apart Hitler's Germany"), and sarcastic retorts ("Shelakhmones Hitlern" or "Purim Gifts for Hitler") set to music by five vocalists and five classical instrumentalists. The compilation was even nominated for a Grammy award.

Tsibele's vocalist and wooden flute

LEFT PHOTO BY OLEG FARYNYUK. RIGHT PHOTO BY PETER HÖNNEMANN.

YidLife Crisis. From left, Jamie Elman and Eli Batalion

player Eléonore Weill wrote the melody to "Dem Nayntn Yanuar" ("The Ninth of January") after finding the song in the same collection of archives from which *Yiddish Glory* culled its songs. "It's an amazing text. It's really passionate and kind of crazy!" exclaims Aqua. But, she continues, "the original melody is really blasé." As a result, the band riled itself musically to match the ferocity of the lyrics depicting the Bloody Sunday march of 1905, with translated lyrics like, "When someone yelled: Jews, Muslims, and Christians / We responded with: Down with capitalism! / Then we, the workers, will raise our heads. / The world will be renewed / when we, the workers, are free."

Music for Everyone

Just like being Christian isn't a prerequisite for enjoying gospel music or Latin hymns, being Jewish isn't required for Yiddish folk song appreciation. The religiosity of any of these bands is also irrelevant to the music they make — both to many of the performers and to many of the listeners they hope to attract. Tsibele's bassist, who Aqua calls "the guru of the band in a lot of ways" is not even Jewish. She

continues, "It's kind of cool seeing what it's like for her to be in a lot of Jewish spaces and answering questions about various weird political aspects of the community."

For Aqua, both the musicality and the Yiddish itself are strong draws. "It's such a flavorful language. There's just so much *geshmahk*, I would say in Yiddish! And then I think when you add in a musical element ... that just adds something," she says. "I think what Tsibele's experienced a lot is Jews and non-Jews just being struck by how Yiddish sounds and being like, 'Wow, that brought out something emotional.' For Jewish people, especially, there's an emotional aspect to just hearing Yiddish that some people don't really expect."

For many Jewish musicians, playing Yiddish folk songs helps connect them spiritually to the traditions of their ancestors or to the *shtetls* of previous generations. But for others, simply finding such revolutionary and relevant secular messages buried within the old texts (especially at a time like this) helps placate what Elman and Batalion so perfectly dubbed the "YidLife Crisis."

And since Yiddish is such a transient language, it continues to evolve and adapt based on geography

and modernity. Music in particular helps facilitate that, Dolgin emphasizes. "If you're Jewish or not, I don't care. But there is something about putting together different styles and different cultures and different languages and places and times ... to show the universality of humanity and that we can all get along. Music is a place where we can all share and learn from each other," he says.

"The Jewish angle is sort of cool for me for people to hear because a lot of people's ideas about Jews are all about synagogues and religions and countries and nation-states ... and there's tons of new anti-Semitism these days that totally freaks me out. It's because of those ideas about Jews, these misconceptions, painting all Jews with one brush. ... So if someone hears one of my songs and is goes, 'What's that weird melody? Oh that's Yiddish? What's Yiddish? Oh, you mean Jews aren't all one thing?' And if you mix up your culture with different cultures, but keep them distinct, too — you don't want to water everything down! — then we can be curious about each other.

"And then," he says, stifling a bashful chuckle, "we can make this world a better place, damn it!" ∎

Lydia Loveless

NO DEPRESSION

Part of the FreshGrass Foundation

No Depression is brought to you by the FreshGrass Foundation, a 501(c)(3) nonprofit organization dedicated to preserving and promoting the past, present, and future of American roots music. In addition to publishing *No Depression* and presenting the annual FreshGrass Festival at Mass MoCA in Western Massachusetts each September, the Foundation funds cash awards for up-and-coming musicians, the No Depression Singer-Songwriter Award, and more. Visit freshgrass.org for more information

Fall 2019: Wellness

The Fall 2019 issue of *No Depression* is our take on a Food & Drink issue. In time for the harvest season, *No Depression* will explore what roots musicians eat, drink, and smoke, as well as farm, foster, and distill. In a larger sense, the issue also aims to balance body and mind and embrace contemporary notions of self-care. Of course, stories will also include a taste of roots music's indulgences, too!

Included in this issue: Aoife O'Donovan, Lydia Loveless, Sarah Shook, Steve Poltz, The Lone Bellow, American Aquarium, Birds of Chicago, Ben Glover

Winter 2019: Vision

No Depression will take a more visual approach to understanding roots music in the Winter 2019 issue. Even though music is primarily an auditory experience, there are so many visual elements that go into presenting, performing, consuming, and engaging with this particular art form. Through *No Depression*'s exceptional print medium, the issue will highlight the photos, comics, graphics, and more that help both musicians and fans see new ideas through the sounds.

NODEPRESSION.COM/SUBSCRIBE

By subscribing to *No Depression*, you're helping support independent media and the future of roots music!

Contributors

ANNE MARGARET DANIEL teaches literature at the New School University in New York City. Since 1989, she has written about books, music, history, and baseball, and most recently is the editor of F. Scott Fitzgerald's *I'd Die For You and Other Lost Stories* (Scribner). Daniel lives in Woodstock, New York, where she is working on books about Fitzgerald and about Bob Dylan.

BEVERLY BRYAN is a writer and former editor of MTV Iggy. Her articles about music have been published in Paste, Remezcla, Noisey, and Spin. She co-hosts a podcast about Latin American indie music called Songmess and resides in Brooklyn.

BONNIE STIERNBERG is a freelance writer based in Brooklyn by way of Chicago, covering music, television, and pop culture. She was formerly music editor at Paste, and recently her work has appeared in Billboard and Rolling Stone.

BRIAN BUTLER is a traveling illustrator and muralist. His endless passion for culture has led him across the state of Massachusetts on an 84-stop mini-golf tour, to the helm of a campaign to elevate anthropomorphic ice cream to the same legendary status as Bigfoot, on a decade-long journey of illustrating more than 2,000 concerts, and on numerous jaunts to paint murals throughout the country.

CHUCK ARMSTRONG is a pastor and writer in New York City. Originally from a town of about 150 people in Northeast Kansas, he lives in Hell's Kitchen with his wife, daughter, and dog.

CARYN ROSE is a New York City-based writer, archivist, and music historian. She is currently at work on *Why Patti Smith Matters* for the University of Texas Press "Music Matters" series.

DUNCAN COOPER is the former editor-in-chief of The Fader and now runs a boutique creative agency called Only Do That Only, with clients across technology and music, including video-sharing platforms, record labels, and prominent recording artists. He lives in the Catskills.

DREW CHRISTIE is a Seattle-based animator and illustrator. His work has been featured by The New York Times, Huffington Post, The Atlantic, and others.

ERIN LYNDAL MARTIN received her MFA in poetry from the University of Alabama. Her work has appeared in The Rumpus, Salon, The Quietus, and elsewhere. Her favorite things are birthday cake and napping with the air conditioner on.

HILARY SAUNDERS is the managing editor at *No Depression* and her previous work has appeared in Paste, ESPN, Next City, The Jewish Daily Forward, and more. She's a proud alumna of the University of Miami and a firm believer that rock and roll can save the world.

JOSHUA M. MILLER is a freelance writer from Wisconsin. His work has been published in a variety of publications, including the Chicago Sun-Times, Milwaukee Magazine, Paste, and Under the Radar.

KATHERINE TURMAN is co-author of the book *Louder Than Hell: The Definitive Oral History of Metal* (HarperCollins) and has produced the syndicated classic rock radio show *Nights with Alice Cooper* since 2006. Her writing has appeared in the Los Angeles Times, Rolling Stone, Billboard, Mother Jones, Esquire.com, Spin, and Village Voice.

KIM KELLY is a writer and labor organizer currently based in New York City. She authors a biweekly labor column for Teen Vogue called "No Class," and her writing on labor, politics, music, and culture has appeared in a multitude of publications, including the New York Times, the Washington Post, the Guardian, the New Republic, Rolling Stone, NPR, and Al Jazeera. She is a proud member and councilperson for the Writers Guild of America, East.

KIM RUEHL was an editor of *No Depression* from 2008 to 2017, bringing the magazine back into print in 2015 and ending her run as editor-in-chief. She has also written for Billboard, NPR, Yes Magazine, and others. She is working on a book about labor and civil rights organizer and folk song collector Zilphia Horton, to be published by the University of Texas Press. She lives in Asheville, North Carolina, with her wife and daughter.

LINFORD DETWEILER is a singer-songwriter, multi-instrumentalist, and one half of the husband-and-wife duo Over The Rhine. Together with his partner Karin Bergquist, Over The Rhine has built a vivid, emotionally charged body of work that has won a devoted following and critical acclaim. The pair is celebrating 30 years of making music together with its 15th studio album, *Love & Revelation*, and their fourth annual Nowhere Else Festival, an intimate gathering that takes place on the Ohio farm they call home.

MARCUS AMAKER is Charleston, South Carolina's first poet laureate and an award-winning graphic designer. His poetry has been featured on PBS Newshour, TEDxCharleston, Alaska Airwaves magazine, and more. His latest book, *empath*, is also an album collaboration with Grammy-nominated musician/producer Quentin E. Baxter of Ranky Tanky.

MARISSA JOHNSON is an illustrator living in Detroit. She finds much of her inspiration in the outdoors and traveling to new places. She specializes in nature illustrations, patterns, illustrated maps, and surface design.

RAYE ZARAGOZA is an award-winning singer-songwriter who has been featured by Billboard, Democracy Now!, and more for her modern-day protest music. Paste named "In The River" the No. 2 Modern Protest Song by a Person of Color. Her debut album, *Fight For You*, seeks to empower others to recognize their own voices and fight for change.

STACY CHANDLER is the assistant editor for *No Depression*. She is a freelance journalist living in Raleigh, North Carolina, with her husband, their daughter, a big dumb yellow dog, and an underused fiddle.

STEFANIE C. FERNÁNDEZ is a music journalist and poet from Miami who is supposed to be from Cuba. Her work has appeared in NPR, Miami New Times, and The Yale Daily News magazine, among others. She currently lives in Washington, D.C., where she is assistant producer for The Atlantic's live team.

WILL HODGE is a Chicago-based journalist who has contributed to Rolling Stone, Paste, CMT Edge, and various other outlets. He is also the editor and community manager for NoiseTrade. When he's not writing about the folk music foundations of classic country and punk rock, he can be found daydreaming about the hip-hop/new wave sonic wonderland of late-'70s/early-'80s NYC.

Screen Door

A PLACE FOR SONGS

BY LINFORD DETWEILER

I'm not 100% sure that I'm a folk musician in any pure sense of the definition. I grew up around plenty of old gospel music, but other than that initial baptism, I never really immersed myself in any one traditional idiom. I feel more like a musical mongrel, a mutt who just happens to love hunting for good songs. But I have come to believe that just about everything that's essential to the formation of folk music —history, place, sustainability, and community — has been essential to my music.

Karin Bergquist and I were small-town Ohio kids. We met at a Quaker liberal arts college where we both studied classical music (although Karin says classical music is just fancy folk music). But what really kept us up at night was the infinite possibility of writing songs of our own.

We migrated to Cincinnati and when we discovered a neighborhood called Over-the-Rhine, we couldn't believe our eyes. It was like someone had picked up a small European city, flown it across the Atlantic Ocean, and dropped it whole near the banks of the Ohio River. I found a third-story apartment right on Main Street between 12th and 13th. Rent was $100 per month — just right for a young aspiring songwriter. I could walk out my front door, look south down Main Street, and see a small piece of the old Riverfront Stadium, home of the Cincinnati Reds, down by the river.

It seemed like we were on sacred ground. There were hints all around us of music that could have only been made in America. Stephen Foster, the father of American songwriting, had lived in Cincinnati as a young man and had walked these same streets. Fats Waller had been the house organist at the historic, almost decrepit Emery Theatre one block away, and he had evolved into a walking jukebox of ragtime, Dixieland, jazz, swing, and stride. Hank Williams, referred to by some as The Hillbilly

Shakespeare, recorded "I'm So Lonesome I Could Cry" just a few blocks west. Were they all somehow beckoning us to join the chorus?

We were starting a band and we needed a name. Maybe nobody would mind if we just borrowed the name of this old neighborhood, this odd prepositional phrase: Over the Rhine.

We recorded our very first handful of songs on a Tascam reel-to-reel 8-track in the spring of 1989. I guess that means for a brief moment, we were an '80s band. Upstairs in my bedroom, I think my hands shook a little as I plugged in my tape recorder and scribbled the first line of the first Over the Rhine song: *Eyes wide open to the great train robbery of my soul ...*

As young writers, Karin and I never relocated to Nashville, or LA, or New York, although we were encouraged from time to time to do just that. I'm sure we missed out on opportunities, and we certainly felt the gravitational pull. But what about all those American writers and artists we were discovering that had a place associated with their work? Flannery O'Connor, Robert Frost, Georgia O'Keeffe, Wendell Berry, Aretha Franklin — they were all from somewhere.

Ohio was our place.

The years passed, and we kept making our music. We kept taking our songs out on the road. We kept trying to

become better writers. In the end, that's the only business plan that matters to an artist: Keep going. You either do or you don't.

And a community of people coalesced around our music. The mailing list we started early on quickly grew to about 10,000 names. We would gather a group of friends together for a week and sit around a table and staple letters together that I had handwritten and photocopied. Postage cost a few thousand dollars. Of course, the old newsletters with licked stamps and handwriting gave way to emails, but we were always curious about the people who were finding our music.

Eventually, Karin and I came to realize we needed a refuge from the road. We wanted something different to return to, a place where we could take a deep breath and hold still. We found a hideaway farm about 45 miles east of Cincinnati, a piece of unpaved earth to call home.

And we couldn't resist inviting our extended musical family to come find us on the farm. We began restoring a barn from the 1870s, turning it into our own music venue. In 2016, we began hosting Nowhere Else Festival every Memorial Day Weekend, inviting some of the great musicians, writers, visual artists, and filmmakers we had met over the years to gather for a weekend of music, art, big skies, some good food, and conversation.

So as I sit in an upstairs bedroom in our old farmhouse, sipping a cup of strong coffee, I think about how 2019 marks the 30th anniversary of Over the Rhine — three whole decades of writing, recording, and life on the road.

It makes me wonder: Am I a folk musician? I'm still not sure. But I know the place I make my music matters. I know that every story begins with those who came before. I know that I play a small part in something big. And good music always brings people together.